LIVIA'S KITCHEN

LIVIA'S KITCHEN

*Naturally Sweet
and Indulgent Treats*

OLIVIA WOLLENBERG

Contents

INTRODUCTION
6

GETTING STARTED
16

STAPLE RECIPES
40

BREAKFAST
62

FLAPJACKS, BROWNIES AND SQUARES
86

BISCUITS AND COOKIES
116

PIES AND TARTS
136

PUDDINGS
156

SWEET BITES
188

CAKES
212

ICE CREAM
236

INDEX
248

INTRODUCTION
The Livia's Kitchen Story

With this book I am welcoming you into my kitchen, my absolute favourite place in the world. I learnt how to cook in this kitchen and some of my happiest memories were made here. From being taught by my Mum to make some of her favourite recipes, to baking cakes and dancing around with my two older sisters, my kitchen holds such a special place in my heart. I feel so lucky to have been able to build a business that revolves around my happy place, and I hope that the ideas that were born here bring huge happiness to lots of you, too.

HOW IT ALL BEGAN

It is hard to know how far back to go in a section titled 'how it all began'. With an extremely vivid memory of my childhood, I'm confident that I could write pages and pages about why the kitchen became my happy place, but I will try to keep it short and sweet! The kitchen in my family home was the central point where we spent most of our time together. It seemed to be the place where we all wanted to be. Going back as far as primary school days, I can remember that my two older sisters and I would do everything in our kitchen – from our homework and playing games to practising instruments – just so that we could keep my Mum company whilst she rustled up something amazing. She used to say that

cooking for the family was her number one pastime, and I really hope it was since she did it almost every night! Even when I was doing my own thing in the kitchen, I was always aware of what my Mum was doing, and wondered how she could create such delicious meals for all of us with such ease.

My Mum says she recognised my love affair with cooking from a really young age, and because of that she spent many hours teaching me basic skills which she said would last me a lifetime. One of the things I was most enthusiastic to learn was how to make a traditional Shabbat dinner. For those of you who don't know, it is a Jewish tradition for families to come together over a big meal on a Friday evening. Although my family are not at all religious, and I don't hold many religious beliefs, what was and always will be important to me is keeping up with the traditions that encourage family time (and, of course, eating). Chicken soup is one of the traditional dishes served at a Friday night dinner, and my Mum's has to be the absolute best in the world. In fact, this was one of the dishes she showed me how to make when I was about ten. Standing on a little stool, I used to peer into the industrial-sized saucepan she insisted on using even when just cooking for the five of us (a classic trait of

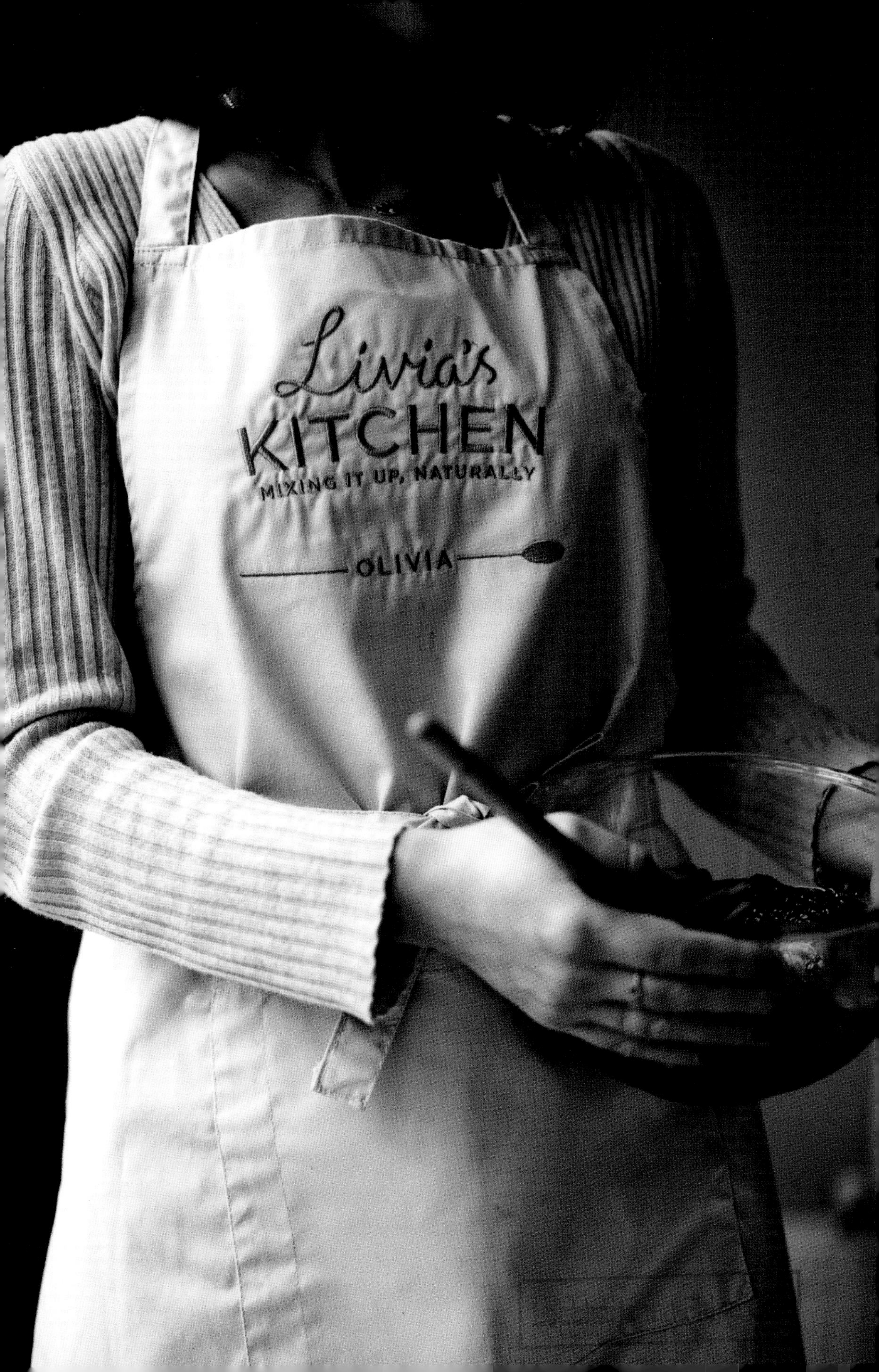
Livia's
KITCHEN
MIXING IT UP, NATURALLY
OLIVIA

a Jewish lady – a chronic fear of underfeeding), and watch carefully whilst she made this magic potion. Her guidelines for making the most delicious, comforting soup will never be forgotten. For that, and for so many other things my Mum has taught me, I am so grateful.

So, my interest in food was always there, and that is why I found it so tough to bring myself to see a nutritionist when I realised that certain foods were making me unwell. I had had a really sensitive stomach since the age of about seventeen, but I had never been able to fully identify what was causing the pain I experienced after eating. In my early twenties, my stomach became increasingly sensitive and I began to feel quite unwell after pretty much every meal. In the new year of 2014, I had had enough. I felt like the pain I experienced after eating was crippling me and interfering with everyday life. So I went to see a qualified nutritionist. The nutritionist only had to take one look at the food diary I had been keeping for two weeks prior to my appointment to identify that I was having problems with a group of foods she called FODMAPs. I had never heard of FODMAPs before. FODMAPs stands for fermentable oligo-saccharides, di-saccharides, monosaccharides and polyols. These FODMAPs are forms of dietary sugars (carbohydrates) which cause problems with digestion and absorption in people with digestive issues. Such people may be put on to a low-FODMAP diet to reduce the presence of these indigestible sugars in the gut, and this is what I was advised to do. A low-FODMAP diet targets certain carbohydrates and so the list isn't as simple as cutting out whole food groups.

Without a doubt, the hardest part of changing my diet was having to cut out the sweet snacks and desserts I used to love so much. Cupcakes with butter icing, jam doughnuts and gooey chocolate cakes were just a few of the many things I used to eat to satisfy my sweet cravings. Being intolerant to wheat and dairy meant I couldn't go near those types of foods anymore. And removing these items from my diet was especially hard because I found that even when I went to health-food shops or supermarkets to find gluten- and dairy-free products, they were often full of artificial preservatives and additives, which I also have to stay away from.

It was around the time of having to revise my diet that other parts of my life were also drastically changing. I had been studying Psychology and Neuroscience at University College London for five years and had loved this academically stimulating subject. However, I started to think that there might be something else out there for me, and that I may be better suited to the world of business, where I would be able to be more creative and socially interactive. In time I thought that nothing would be better than combining business with my love for cooking and new passion for healthy eating and living, which had arisen from having to change my diet. Deciding to leave neuroscience behind and embark on a completely new career wasn't an easy decision, but once I had chosen to go with my idea, I was immediately committed to it and hugely excited by the prospect and lifestyle change. The challenge was on!

It didn't take me long to identify what it was that I wanted to do. Based on my own experiences and problems in finding good and wholesome sweet snacks, I decided that I wanted to set up a company that made these sorts of foods accessible, delicious and fun.

After many late nights experimenting in the kitchen, and with guidance from a nutritionist, I decided to launch with a range of deliciously nutritious crumbles. Why crumbles? Firstly, I was starting a company from scratch and no one had heard of me. For this reason I thought it was really important to bring out a product that people knew and loved, although my version of it would be completely unique. Secondly, although crumbles are a quintessential British dessert, there was no other company producing a range of healthy crumbles. Most importantly, I chose crumbles because there were many ways to make them both delicious and nutritious.

In the summer of 2014, I took the idea of making comfort foods with a nutritional twist on an eight-week intensive business course at UCL, in which I was taught the fundamentals of starting a business and where I had to pitch for funding at the end of the course. I won this competition and a significant grant, which gave me the confidence and resources to start pitching to big retailers. These retailers not only loved the concept, but also the taste. Selfridges was the first store to sell Livia's Kitchen Crumbles. I had always loved the Selfridges Food Hall and it felt so magically surreal to be making the crumbles in my kitchen, and then to visit Selfridges and see them on the shelves. It was an incredible feeling!

Even when the orders steadily increased, and the number of stockists increased, too, I made the decision to keep production in my kitchen for as long as it made sense. Working from my kitchen was giving me such pleasure, and I felt strongly about continuing to produce from there for stage one of my business so that initial members of staff could understand my core values, where they had originated and why the kitchen was so important to me. When orders increased, I didn't look at moving out, I just looked to bring in more help.

And this is the part where I explain how my company grew from one (me) to a small dedicated team (my 'kitchen elves') in a number of months. By December 2014, I recognised that I was beginning to 'crumble' under the pressure of the business. Not only was I still doing all the baking, but I was also doing the deliveries and distribution, and everything else involved in running a business. When I first started employing people, I have to say that I found it really hard. I initially had the view that explaining what and how things needed to be done would take more time than just doing it myself, and I felt somewhat cautious of taking people in. However, I quite quickly learned the art of delegation and how important it is. I know the whole process was made a lot easier because of the quality of my elves. With only a few thousand Instagram followers at that time, I put an advert on my page for an intern and some people to help me in the kitchen. I was stunned by the response, and interviewed at least ten people, all of whom seemed wonderful and passionate about what I was doing. I had to really choose carefully, though, as it was important to consider that I was inviting these people into my family home, which perhaps is not the most conventional of work set-ups! I also put an advert up in Leiths cookery school and found two very skilled, enthusiastic chefs who came for work experience with me over the Christmas period. I started calling my helpers 'elves' at this time, since they were helping me to bake hundreds of Christmas Crumbles, and the name just stuck.

Over time, the most amazing army of kitchen elves was built, and I truly feel as if I can call all of them my friends. In the first year of the business, two of these girls, Emma and Lydia, became full-time staff and they are now an integral part of the company. We have experienced our fair share of tears, stress and emotion together, but above it all we have become a strong team and I know that they will do everything to make my company a success. I had thought that inviting people into my home might be challenging, but it never was. The girls are always incredibly mindful, and I think they really warmed to the fact that the environment was relaxed and social. On the bake days when the crumbles were being made, Emma and I would work on our laptops in the living room and we could hear the sounds of all the elves talking, laughing and crumbling away in the kitchen – it was always so happy.

You may be wondering at this point in the story how my parents felt about their home becoming a factory and office. Well, they were unswervingly supportive and welcoming, and they never for a second seemed to begrudge how it was all operating. My Mum happily accepted that she wouldn't be able to use her kitchen that much, which can't have been easy for her. And not only was the kitchen out of bounds, but we took over other rooms, too. My sisters' old rooms were used for storage, the living room became my office, and our hallway was filled with the monstrosity of the shrink-wrapper machine (individually sealing each crumble). My parents did not just facilitate the growth of the company by giving up their home for a year or so, but they also contributed to it by offering me endless advice and support. The encouragement that both of them provide to me every day makes me even more determined to make a success of what I have built so far.

Although working from my family home was such a pleasure, I recognised (and hoped) that the demand for my products would be too high to maintain from a home kitchen, and so I started looking for a factory that would be able to manufacture the Livia's Kitchen products for me. This was a long and complicated process as my products have so many different requirements; all of the elements that make up the products posed difficulties for the majority of factories. However, towards the end of 2015 I finally found a wonderful factory that wanted to support and help me with the new items I wished to focus on.

Without question, one of the main reasons I adore what I am doing so much is because of the nature of the other people working in this industry. The information I have received from others in the health-food world has been essential. What is extraordinary about this industry is that no one views anyone else primarily as competition. We all see each other as people spreading the same message in our own unique way, and that the more of us out there, the better. People within this industry have become some of my closest friends and

I am so grateful to them all for welcoming me into their community and offering up their experiences when I was starting out.

So... how was I given the opportunity to write a cookbook? Well, after the amazing response and uptake of the Livia's Kitchen Crumble, and the interest from people globally in what I was doing, I felt encouraged to continue my experimentation with sweet yet healthy treats. I feel so passionately about doing this because after only two months of eliminating certain food groups from my diet and sticking to foods that offer nutritional benefits, I felt much stronger and healthier. This book was written so that I could share my love of healthy eating and to show that it doesn't have to be difficult or expensive and it can be totally delicious, too.

Once I started developing the recipes for the book, I quickly realised how great they would be for so many different types of people and for all ages. The simplicity of the recipes ensures that they are suitable for young children to make with the help of their parents, and some are even perfect for them to make on their own. I hope that this book encourages a better way of providing treats to children and makes baking more accessible to them from an early age.

Although all the recipes in this book are wheat- and dairy-free due to the way in which I eat, I recognise that everyone is different. If you are someone, for example, who feels absolutely fine with dairy, then dairy products such as milk can be used as a substitute for the ingredients I have used in their place. It is all about nourishing your body in the way it deserves. I feel so happy to have found a way to continue eating everything I love whilst feeling better than ever before. Life is sweet – eat it and love it.

Getting Started

WHY I EAT WHAT I EAT
and My Favourite Ingredients

It was in April 2014 that I made changes to my diet. My stomach had become sensitive at around the age of 17 after suffering from quite a severe case of glandular fever. My liver was affected by the condition and I was never able to digest really fatty, oily foods after that. Cheese, alcohol and fatty meats were foods I could easily identify as ones that did not agree with me. However, even when I tried to stay away from these foods, I would often still feel really unwell after eating. I absolutely hated that this happened, but because I was a lover of pretty much every food type, I put off going to see someone about my troubles for years. As time went on, though, I increasingly began to experience problems, and the pain after eating most meals became so severe that I knew something had to change.

Thankfully, I was given the all clear from the doctors and was reassured that I had nothing dangerous going on internally. However, the nutritionists and dieticians I saw after that identified that I was extremely intolerant to and unable to digest quite a large variety of foods. The nutritionist I visited put me on the FODMAP plan, where for six weeks a whole host of food groups were eliminated and then slowly reintroduced to determine which foods I could and could not eat going forwards.

I did not digest well (excuse the pun) the idea of cutting out wheat, dairy and many other food groups from my diet. I assumed that if these groups were eliminated, my diet would become restrictive and boring. But I was left with little choice as I had started to experience so much pain, so I fully committed to this new regime and began my six-week challenge. When one starts the FODMAP diet the aim is that, after the six-week period, foods are reintroduced slowly in order to identify where the problems lie. In my case, when I tried to re-introduce foods into my diet, I appeared to be intolerant to the large majority of them. Wheat, dairy, certain preservatives, certain beans, onions and garlic are just some of the foods I had to cut out. I knew this was going to result in a massive readjustment of my life, but by the time the six-week period was up, I had already begun to feel so much better physically, and so the idea of having to make changes seemed more exciting than scary.

Due to my persistent sweet cravings it was important for me to learn how to satisfy my sweet tooth in a different way to how I had before. I learned all about natural sweeteners, such as dates and maple syrup, and had such fun experimenting with these and other new ingredients whilst baking. In order to never go back to eating in the way I once did, it was crucial that my diet consisted of delicious, wholesome food so that I never had to feel as if I was on a diet. It is really important to listen to your body, and when my sweet cravings hit I don't like to ignore them! Satisfying sweet cravings with these new ingredients was exciting because I learned that they can offer nutritional benefits whilst maintaining and boosting energy levels – rather than causing the energy crashes that I was so used to. Almost immediately after changing my diet, I stopped having these crashes, and I felt so much more able to keep active, strong and focused since I was restored with energy. Not only did my energy levels improve, but my hair, skin and general mood did, too.

So, it is for these reasons that I try to keep to what is often referred to as a 'clean' diet. I am not inclined, however, to describe this way of eating as 'clean' as I feel it denotes some type of rigidity and restriction, and my diet is certainly not either of those! I do exclude all gluten, wheat, dairy and refined sugar from my diet, but I focus very much on what it is going into my body and the benefits it provides me with, rather than worrying and concerning myself with what I cannot eat and with calorie counting. With the growth of the health-food market and the choice of 'free-from' products, I notice that so many people buy into products when they have a free-from label on them and often miss the huge list of additives that they may contain. Just because something is labelled 'gluten-free' does not necessarily guarantee it contains good and healthy ingredients. Of course someone with allergies or intolerances must focus on what a product is free from, but I

believe it is equally important to focus on what the food is made with.

I chose to be wheat-, gluten- and dairy-free because it made me feel better in myself. I know that many others share all or some of these intolerances and so I wanted to create a world of possibilities for us. Others may only have one or even no intolerances, but are still interested in eating in a different, and perhaps more natural, way. Some of you, for example, may know your bodies well enough to know that dairy is not a problem food, and therefore you may choose to incorporate it in these recipes.

I hope that this book can show that refined ingredients are not necessary and, in fact, that natural foods can create the most delicious, indulgent treats. Of course, everything should still be enjoyed in moderation (although I sometimes find this really difficult to follow when I want to eat everything in my mixing bowl). Whilst I only use good and natural ingredients, this does not necessarily mean you should eat unlimited amounts of them!

There are often complaints about the nature of the 'healthy food world' being predominantly nut based and nut heavy. I have tried my very best in this book to shake this conception a little by including many nut-free recipes. I hope this means that there is something in this book for everyone, as I never liked the idea of people with nut allergies or intolerances having to stay away.

Since I am aware that many people like to adapt recipes, I have created a chapter of staple recipes that can be referred to at all times. If, for example, someone has a nut allergy and I suggest a nutty pie base for a tart, then that can be substituted for one of the other two pie bases that are in that section. This book has allowed me to be my most creative self, and I hope that it enables you to be creative, too, so that you can make my recipes and tweak them to suit you.

It is important to me that the nutritional benefits of the main ingredients used throughout this book are well understood. So here I will talk you through my store cupboard and explain why it is that I love to use its ingredients. My nutritionist has helped me to write the following section.

My beloved coconut and its derivatives

COCONUT OIL

HEALTH BENEFITS:
Coconut oil is now commonly recognised as one of nature's most nourishing foods and its health benefits are well documented. They range from healthy hair and skin to improved digestion and increased immune function. Coconut oil is made up of healthy fats, which contain antifungal, antibacterial and antiviral properties and which, when combined with a well-balanced diet and eaten in moderation, can help boost our immune system. It has also been shown to increase the speed of thyroid function, which can help with weight control and toxin elimination. For those of you who (like me!) suffer with digestive disorders, coconut oil can also be quite effective in soothing discomfort.

All these properties also make coconut oil an incredible natural beauty product. It can be used as a facial and body moisturiser, as a cream to soothe sunburns, nourish damaged hair – and much more. A tip when purchasing coconut oil is that to get the most out of it, it should be raw and cold-pressed. This kind of oil will have both a strong flavour and fragrance to it. Raw coconut oil is made from fresh raw coconut meat/flesh, which is dried out in a controlled environment. This ensures it is not heated above a certain point, which enables the coconut meat to retain its many nutrients. Buying cold-pressed coconut oil means that the dried coconut is not processed above a certain temperature, which again ensures its goodness. Accessible brands that make this type of oil are Biona and Lucy Bee.

HOW TO USE IT:
As a baking ingredient, coconut oil can be used to replace butter, as it is a malleable fat, and also sometimes it can be used as a replacement for eggs, as it helps to bind ingredients. It will add a rich creaminess and a lovely tropical flavour. When it comes to cooking, coconut oil has a higher smoking temperature than most polyunsaturated or monounsaturated oils, so it is ideal when you require high cooking temperatures as it can withstand these without becoming rancid and releasing trans fats, which contribute to high cholesterol and cardiovascular-related diseases.

It is important to note that coconut oil can be used as a solid or a liquid. Using soft (but still solid) coconut oil will allow for a mixture to be firmer than one in which melted coconut oil is used. As a general rule, in raw recipes I tend to use soft solid coconut oil to help bind ingredients. In recipes that require baking, I use melted coconut oil so that it easily spreads through the mix and works more like a butter.

not raw, and therefore does not contain quite as much goodness, however it can be ideal in baking and cooking if you don't want your recipe to taste at all like coconut. Although this type of oil is not as nutritionally valuable as the raw alternative, I do tend to use it in recipes because taste is as important to me as nutrition, and sometimes a recipe will just work better when there is no coconut taste. There are other types of coconut oils available that are odourless and tasteless, but sometimes they can be overly processed and have an unpleasant flavour, and so I would always recommend using a higher-quality one like Biona, where the oil has just been lightly steamed.

COCONUT BUTTER

HEALTH BENEFITS:
The nutritional benefits of coconut butter are similar to those of coconut oil, except the butter contains valuable fibre from the coconut flesh, bringing you the best of both worlds when it comes to total nourishment.

HOW TO USE IT:
Coconut butter is another great alternative to ordinary butter. I even use it when greasing my baking tins. I use Biona's coconut butter, which is almost like a creamed coconut. In my recipes, when coconut butter is used, coconut oil could be used in its place, but do remember that the final result may not be as firm at room temperature, although generally it will be absolutely fine.

Do remember that when using coconut oil in a recipe the final product will have an ingredient in it that will firm up when refrigerated. So a cake, for example, which has coconut oil in it will have a different texture when kept in the fridge to when it is stored at room temperature. You can purposefully use coconut oil in a recipe when you want something to firm when chilled.

I use two different types of coconut oils; the brand I most commonly use for both is made by Biona. Biona produce a raw organic coconut oil, which has a delicious coconut flavour and smell, and can provide a recipe with a lovely subtle tropical flavour. They also produce a type of coconut oil called Cuisine, which has been lightly steamed to reduce the strong coconut flavour and taste. This type of coconut oil is

DESICCATED COCONUT

HEALTH BENEFITS:

Desiccated coconut is simply fresh coconut meat that has been grated and dried. It is rich in dietary fibre, iron, manganese, copper and selenium. Desiccated coconut is a great source of iron for vegans who are at risk of iron-deficiency anaemia.

HOW TO USE IT:

I use desiccated coconut to add an extra coconut flavour to my recipes and to give a mixture a nice little extra bite. Adding too much of it, however, can make the finished texture quite dry and chewy, so just be careful not to overdo it! I also love to use desiccated coconut as a garnish on many of my recipes. A sprinkling on top of a treat can make anything look beautiful.

COCONUT FLOUR

HEALTH BENEFITS:

Coconut flour is made from fresh coconut meat that is dried at low temperatures and then ground into a fine flour. It is a great gluten-free flour and is a perfect alternative if you suffer from either digestive problems or nut allergies. It is a wonderful option if you are unable to consume other types of flours, such as wheat, gluten or nut-containing flours. Coconut flour is also bursting with fibre and protein and it's a really good low-glycaemic alternative that does not spike blood sugar levels as quickly as grain-based flours.

HOW TO USE IT:

This flour has a naturally sweet taste and therefore allows you to use less sweetener in a recipe. It is ideal for people who stick to a paleo diet and are unable to eat flours made from grains, and also for those who are nut-free and so cannot eat nut flours. When I use coconut flour I sift it because otherwise the texture is slightly bitty. Used in the right quantities, coconut flour can create a lighter texture than oat and buckwheat flours. It also absorbs a lot of liquid, so recipes using it often call for more binding ingredients such as flax egg (see page 32) or banana. I use Biona's coconut flour.

COCONUT MILK

HEALTH BENEFITS:

Coconut milk, as with all natural derivatives of coconut, boasts many essential vitamins and minerals. It also contains a significant amount of vitamins C and E. The unique fatty acids in coconut milk can help improve immune function, reduce the risk of heart disease and improve skin and hair health.

HOW TO USE IT:

I don't tend to use coconut milk as a straight dairy milk replacement as it has a strong coconut taste and therefore can be quite overpowering. I wouldn't put it in my tea or with granola, for example! However, I do use it as a dairy replacement in some recipes as it provides a great creaminess. The large majority of coconut milks have additives and preservatives, so I use Biona's full-fat coconut milk, which is completely natural.

OATS

HEALTH BENEFITS:

Oats have the most soluble fibre of all grains and are an excellent source of slow-releasing carbohydrates, which will give you energy to tackle a busy day. They contain a fibre known as beta-glucan, which has been extensively studied for its health benefits, including its ability to lower cholesterol and stabilize blood sugar levels. Oats are also high in antioxidants that help keep the heart healthy and are a rich source of vitamin E (which is great for skin), zinc, selenium, copper and magnesium. They also add a good source of protein, particularly if you're vegan.

There is often confusion about whether you can eat oats if you are following a gluten-free diet. Oats are a naturally gluten-free grain. They contain a protein called avenin, which is similar to gluten, but not the same. Most people with coeliac disease are able to eat oats safely. In the shops, certified gluten-free oats are now easily accessible. These oats have absolutely nothing different about them, other than being guaranteed to have been packaged in an accredited gluten-free facility whereby any cross-contamination with gluten cannot occur. For people who react really badly to gluten, it is recommended that they stick to these gluten-free oats to avoid any risk of contamination. Although I am intolerant to gluten, I tend to use mainstream oats and never have any negative side-effects.

HOW TO USE THEM:

Well, this list could be extensive. I absolutely adore oats and use them in a large number of my recipes. Not only are they a wonderful ingredient in their full form, but they can also be made into a flour and a milk, too!

In my recipes, I either use jumbo oats or rolled oats. They have similar tastes and functions, but rolled oats act a little more like a flour since they are finer and less structured than jumbo oats. I also mainly use rolled oats for oat milk, as they make a slightly thicker milk than jumbo oats when you are not using a food processor, and allow for a quicker process of milk-making. Rolled oats can also be used in any recipe where you don't want oats to be chunky and dominating.

OAT FLOUR

Oats do not have a strong taste, so oat flour is great to use. It can thicken a recipe and make the results quite dense. To make oat flour at home, simply grind jumbo or rolled oats in a food processor until a flour is formed. For a really fine, powdery consistency, use a fine-mesh sieve. A fine flour is ideal for pastry as it makes the mixture smoother. Oat flour can be bought, and I tend to keep a few bags of Bob's Red Mill flour in my cupboard for convenience. However, it can be quite expensive, so grinding your own oats might make more sense.

OAT MILK

This can be used as a replacement for normal dairy milk. The thickness of oat milk depends on how long you soak the oats for. Thick oat milk can be used to replace cream and I use this in my custard. Oat milk is also a healthier alternative for people on a dairy-free diet consuming a lot of soya. If not making my own, I tend to buy Oatly organic oat drink, which has no additives or preservatives.

BUCKWHEAT GROATS

HEALTH BENEFITS:

Buckwheat groats come from the seed of a plant that is technically not a grain at all! Buckwheat is energising, nutritious and packed with fibre, which can help you feel fuller for longer and prevent a spike in your blood sugar levels. It is also a good source of magnesium, which is essential for improving blood flow and delivering nutrients, while lowering blood pressure. And it also provides huge support to the liver – all amazing for a healthy cardiovascular system.

HOW TO USE THEM:

I love to use buckwheat groats in some of my raw recipes as they provide a great crunch! They work so well in raw granola bars, for example, as groats are a brilliant nutritional boost in the morning.

BUCKWHEAT FLOUR

HEALTH BENEFITS:

Refined flours provide far fewer nutritional benefits than an unrefined flour such as buckwheat. Grains that are refined before milling lose their germ and bran, which means that as much as 50 per cent of their B vitamins and minerals as well as their vitamin E content are lost. In cases where the bran is completely removed, almost all of the fibre content is lost, too. Alternative unrefined flours are now widely available and are an excellent source of nutrients.

HOW TO USE IT:

Buckwheat flour can be used as an alternative to refined flours. It has quite a distinct taste, and so I generally use it in recipes that contain other ingredients that have strong flavours so that the buckwheat is more subtle.

CACAO POWDER

HEALTH BENEFITS:

Raw cacao is often referred to as a 'superfood' because of its numerous health benefits. Unlike regular cocoa powder, raw cacao is made by cold-pressing cocoa beans to remove the fat without killing the living enzymes. Cacao is an excellent source of magnesium, which helps heart function and brain power whilst increasing the body's alkalinity. It is also rich in antioxidants, iron, chromium, zinc and sulphur, all of which help to keep the skin beautifully healthy. Chromium also plays a role in preventing sugar cravings.

It is for all of these reasons that chocolate is often said to be so good for you, but it is important to note that it is chocolate in the form of cacao that offers these benefits, not store-bought chocolate, which is usually made from refined cacao (cocoa) and mixed with other ingredients, such as refined sugars and condensed milk. One last fact about cacao that I love is that it is a natural mood booster since it stimulates oxytocin, the same chemicals in the brain that are released when we experience feelings of love. What could be better?!

HOW TO USE IT:

Cacao powder is the form of cacao most commonly used in my recipes, but it can also be found as cacao butter and as nibs. I use cacao powder more than the other two forms because it is a really versatile ingredient in baking. Not only does cacao powder add a deep, rich, chocolatey flavour, but it can also act as a

flour, helping in binding and drying out a wet mixture. Cacao butter, on the other hand, is used to make raw chocolate, which I love! Cacao nibs can be used to give a recipe a little extra crunch and bite, but often they can be quite bitter so I don't use them regularly.

One thing I have noticed when making raw chocolate is how much the flavour of cacao butter varies between brands. For this reason, I tend to stick with Choc Chick as I have found this to be the sweetest and least bitter of the ones I have tried.

ALMONDS

HEALTH BENEFITS:

The list of health benefits of almonds is extensive. Almonds are composed of mono-unsaturated fats, which are commonly referred to as 'healthy fats'. These are known for helping decrease high levels of 'bad' cholesterol in the body, making them a very heart-friendly snack. The potassium level present in almonds helps to regulate blood pressure. Almonds are rich in fibre, which assists a healthy digestive system and contributes to the sensation of being full. By munching away on almonds you can top up on important minerals: manganese, which helps the body form strong bones and regulate blood sugar, and magnesium, which is essential for muscle and nerve function and blood sugar control. They are also a very good source of calcium (again this is an important calcium alternative if you're vegan and abstain from dairy), which is important in promoting strong and healthy bones. They are low in sugar and high in protein – the perfect balance to keep you energised throughout the day.

HOW TO USE THEM:

This list is as extensive as the list of health benefits! Since changing my diet and cutting out wheat and dairy, almonds have become a favourite ingredient of mine, not just because of their taste and nutritional qualities, but also due to their versatility in baking and cooking, where they can be used to make recipes like pie bases and energy balls. Almonds can be bought in a variety of different forms. I always buy raw almonds or blanched almonds. I stay away from buying roasted nuts because of the amount of salt and oil often added to them and also because in this form many of their beneficial nutritional properties are also destroyed. Blanched almonds are natural almonds that have been boiled very quickly so that the skin is removed. I like to use blanched almonds in most of my baking for a couple of reasons. Firstly because they allow for a paler, more even-coloured mix, and secondly they are slightly less bitter without the skins on.

ALMOND BUTTER

These days, almond butter made with 100 per cent almonds is not a difficult ingredient to buy, although it can be quite expensive. It is made by simply grinding the almonds in a food processor for approximately 15–20 minutes. The nuts go through several steps from whole to pieces to powder before the fats they contain form a butter. Almond butter can be made with both raw and blanched almonds, and these will have very different colours (the blanched almond butter being a lot paler).

Almond butter has a high satiety value, meaning it keeps you fuller for longer (and a little bit goes a long way). It can be used as a replacement for normal butter as it acts in the same way by providing a fat and helping to bind a mixture. Almond butter also adds a great rich taste to mixtures. Almond butter can be made at home in a strong food processor, but for convenience and because I love to eat it and use it in recipes so much, I often buy large tubs of it from Meridian so that I always have some in my cupboard.

ALMOND MILK

This is such a great alternative to normal milk and can be used to directly replace milk in a recipe. It can also add moisture to a mix, making a thinner, lighter consistency.

Almond milk is really simple to make and home-made almond milk is my absolute favourite as it has so much flavour and I know it is really fresh. It does take some forward planning, though, as the nuts need to be soaked in advance, so I tend to always keep a carton of Rude Health almond milk in my fridge, too.

ALMOND FLOUR/MEAL/GROUND

This is made by blending whole almonds in a food processor for 1–2 minutes until a powder-like substance is formed. For a finer flour, it is best to use blanched almonds because grinding almonds with their skins still on will result in a coarser texture. Almond flour can be used instead of refined flours, although it must be considered that it is heavier and more flavoursome so is often used in smaller quantities. Ground almonds are accessible in the shops, but it is often cheaper to make your own at home.

HOW TO USE IT:

When almonds are ground into pieces, some of their fat is released and the pieces become quite naturally sticky. Combined with dates this allows for a gooey, wholesome mix that binds well. It is also interesting to note that the body absorbs less of the healthy fats from almonds in their whole form than when chopped or broken down into flour or butter.

PECANS

HEALTH BENEFITS:

Pecans are another group of nuts that offer a number of benefits to our overall health. The protein contained in most nuts helps with cell regeneration and muscle building, but pecans are also very rich in vitamin E, which plays an antioxidant role in cell protection, anti-inflammation and heart disease prevention, making it a very 'heart-friendly' nut! Pecans are packed with minerals such as copper, critical for energy production; magnesium, which helps maintain a healthy immune system and nerve function; and zinc, great for immunity and wound healing as well as manganese. Pecans are also rich in calcium, iron and selenium – safe to say they are a nutrition powerhouse!

HOW TO USE THEM:

Pecans have a distinct taste and add a deep, nutty flavour to many recipes. They work in the same way as almonds in that by blending them in a food processor you can make pecan pieces, flour and butter. I use pecans over almonds when I want a recipe to have a richer, nuttier flavour. Using pecan pieces in a recipe allows for great textures and crunch!

PECAN FLOUR

This is made by blending whole pecans in a food processor for 1–2 minutes until a powder-like substance is formed. This can be used as an alternative for refined flours, to thicken a mix or to give a recipe a nutty flavour.

PECAN BUTTER

This type of nut butter is not easily found in stores but is so easy to make at home. By blending the pecans past the point of a flour it will eventually turn into butter. You can try this instead of normal butter in a recipe, although it is dense and so less of it is needed.

CASHEWS

HEALTH BENEFITS:

Cashews are high in antioxidants and oleic acid, which can promote cardiovascular health. They are also rich in the copper and magnesium that aid the strengthening of hair and bones. Cashews have a lower fat content compared to other nuts and are full of fibre, so can be a great snack when wanting to manage weight gain.

HOW TO USE THEM:

When I use cashews in a recipe, I most commonly pre-soak them overnight. I use cashews when I want to create a creamy consistency, and by soaking them in cool water and then blending them, a creamy texture is formed. Cashews have more of a subtle flavour, so when other ingredients are added to this creamy mix, the taste of the nuts is very subtle, allowing for the other flavours to come through. When soaked cashews are blended and mixed with water and coconut oil, it sets very well in the freezer, which results in an ice-cream- or cheesecake-like texture.

MACA POWDER

HEALTH BENEFITS:

Maca is a root vegetable native to the Peruvian Andes and it has been known as the 'Peruvian Ginseng' for its many health benefits, which make it a perfect food supplement. Maca powder, when used in combination with a healthy diet, provides a good source of iron, calcium and protein. Maca is also rich in vitamins B, C and E. It is widely used to correct hormonal imbalances, including menstrual and menopausal disorders. Maca can also work towards supporting a healthy immune system, the endocrine system and thyroid function. Most commonly, maca is used for increasing energy levels, which can help to promote a more active lifestyle.

HOW TO USE IT:

Maca is a go-to ingredient for me and I love to use it in my baking. Being in powdered form means it is versatile and easy to incorporate into my recipes. When maca is mixed with maple syrup, it gives an amazingly rich, caramel-like flavour, which I absolutely love. Maca powder has a really strong and unique taste, and so not much of it has to be used. I use Naturya Maca Powder; I typically buy Naturya branded products for all superfood powders I need.

MATCHA POWDER

HEALTH BENEFITS:

Matcha is green tea in its purest form and contains 50 times more antioxidants than green tea. Antioxidants are essential for removing free radicals from the body, which are produced by the stress of daily life, pollution and exercise. Matcha also supports the immune system, aids digestion and stimulates the metabolism. It is great to use in cakes or energy balls.

QUINOA

HEALTH BENEFITS:

Quinoa is often referred to as 'the mother grain' because of its extraordinarily dense nutrient composition and health-boosting properties. Quinoa is a pseudo grain; this means it is commonly perceived as a grain, but is actually a seed related to beetroot, chard and spinach. Its most famous property is that it is the only plant food that supplies a complete protein profile, offering all eight essential amino acids. Essential amino acids are ones that the body cannot produce on its own and must therefore be consumed through a balanced and varied diet. Besides this, it is packed with protein and has much higher quantities of fibre than most other grains. Quinoa is also full of iron, which is essential to keep our red blood cells healthy, as well as being rich in magnesium, which is vital to relax blood vessels and promote healthy blood sugar control.

HOW TO USE IT:

This is such a simple ingredient, which is now easily accessible and can be bought in a variety of forms. I use plain quinoa and quinoa pops. When cooked, plain quinoa is soft and fluffy, with a slightly nutty taste. It is ideal to use in cooking as an alternative to gluten-containing flours or grains, and I love to have it for breakfast as a porridge substitute. Simply mix with ingredients such as mashed banana and you can make a delicious, simple and satisfying breakfast in minutes! Quinoa pops/puffs are puffed quinoa and I like to use these when making fun sweet treats such as maca quinoa crispies. They can also be used to make a type of quinoa flour when broken down in a food processor. I use this flour to make a pie crust.

FLAXSEEDS (FLAXSEED EGG)

HEALTH BENEFITS:

Don't be fooled by the size of this tiny seed – flaxseeds may be small but they are packed with an incredible range of nutrients. They are rich in most B-complex vitamins and vitamin E, as well as minerals such as magnesium, potassium and iron. Vitamin E is essential for healthy skin. Potassium maintains nerve health, muscle contraction and body fluid control, and iron is a vital component of red blood cells. They are also packed with fibre, making them an easy addition to your diet if you suffer from constipation. Flaxseeds are one of the most concentrated plant sources of omega-3 fats, which are known for their anti-inflammatory and disease-fighting properties. Omega 3 is also essential for cognitive function.

HOW TO USE THEM:

These seeds have a lovely light, discreet nutty flavour that blends very nicely in many of my recipes. Flax can be added to recipes for a nutritional boost, but can also be used in the form of a flax egg to assist in binding ingredients. By simply adding water to flaxseeds and letting them sit for 10 minutes, a flax egg is made. In many recipes, this can be used as a replacement for a normal egg. Flax eggs are a great alternative as they are also high in protein. To make a flax egg, use 1 tablespoon flaxseed to 2–3 tablespoons water and leave to sit for a while to get sticky.

SWEETENERS AND FRUIT

Sugar seems to be the hot topic at the moment and it is becoming common knowledge that refined white sugar has devastating effects on our health. The truth is, sugar is everywhere and it is quite hard to avoid. However, it provides our body with 'empty calories' as it offers no nutritional value. It also has a negative impact on our blood sugar levels, which increases our cravings, meaning we eat more of it. This becomes a vicious circle that is difficult to break.

Our bodies are naturally programmed to enjoy sweet tastes. Having a 'sweet tooth' is one of the most natural human instincts. The problem is, our bodies were not designed to cope with the amount of refined sugars that today's society is consuming at such an alarmingly increasing rate. From personal experience, I know that battling a sweet tooth is not easy, and I found it particularly difficult when my diet drastically changed. This is one of the reasons why Livia's Kitchen was created – I wanted people to be able to satisfy their sweet cravings in a totally different way.

What is sugar?

Sugar is a carbohydrate. Carbohydrates are macronutrients in foods that provide energy to our bodies. The type of carbohydrate we eat affects the type of impact on our health. While carbohydrates are commonly classified into simple and complex, they can also be categorized as refined or unrefined.

Refined carbohydrates are ones that have been processed or altered with the addition of artificial chemicals and sugars, and their natural nutrients such as fibres, vitamins and minerals have been reduced or eliminated.

Unrefined carbohydrates are in their natural state and they contain all the naturally occurring nutrients that are beneficial to the body. These tend to be high in fibre, which is responsible for maintaining healthy blood sugar levels and helps with appetite control as it keeps you fuller for longer. This makes my recipes healthier, and therefore they are a better way to enjoy the sweeter things in life.

However, even given the sweet perks of natural sweeteners, the same rule should apply as with all sugar-based sweeteners: if you're going to consume them, make sure you do so in moderation! My recipes combine a balance of sweetness from fresh fruits, dried fruits, added maple syrup and other naturally sweet foods. Yes, natural sweeteners do contain sugar, but they are a healthier alternative to refined white sugar.

My favourite unrefined sugars to use

MAPLE SYRUP

HEALTH BENEFITS:
Maple syrup is prepared using the sugary sap from the maple tree. Pure maple syrup contains a variety of trace minerals, such as small amounts of calcium, iron, magnesium, potassium, zinc, copper and manganese. These minerals play essential roles in the body,

including cell formation and tissue repair, immune support, keeping bones and teeth strong and regulating muscle contractions.

HOW TO USE IT:

Look for a bottle that lists pure maple syrup as its only ingredient. Maple syrup is a sweetener that doesn't overpower a mixture with its taste. It brings out the flavour of many ingredients, making the deliciousness of recipes slightly more intense. What is great about using maple syrup as opposed to a crystallised sugar is that it is a liquid and helps to thin and bind many ingredients. Not only can maple syrup be used in recipes, but it can also be drizzled over ingredients. Nothing beats a stack of pancakes with a drizzle of maple syrup!

DATES

HEALTH BENEFITS:

Dates are an excellent source of dietary fibre, which is crucial for a healthy digestive system, and they also help to lower blood cholesterol levels. Dates are easily digested, allowing our bodies to make full use of their goodness and energy. They contain a variety of antioxidants with great anti-inflammatory properties. They are also a great source of iron and potassium. Potassium makes up part of both cell and body fluids that aid in controlling blood pressure. Dates are also rich in minerals such as calcium, manganese, copper and magnesium.

HOW TO USE THEM:

Dates are an ingredient I use for a number of reasons. Not only can they be used as a sweetener, but also to bind ingredients, especially in raw cooking/baking. I also commonly use dates in recipes involving grains that need mixing in a food processor. Medjool dates are the best type of date to use in my recipes as they are generally much softer and gluier than other types, which helps them act as a binding agent when needed. If you buy Medjool dates that are hard, it is not a problem at all, but you should always soak them in hot water for 10 minutes before using. This softens the dates and allows them to be mixed into a recipe with more ease. Always make sure to pit your dates before using. The stones can break a food processor and are not nice to eat!

DATE SYRUP

Date syrup is made by extracting the juice from dates. The syrup this forms is a dark, rich colour and adds a deep sweetness to recipes. Only small amounts of date syrup need to be used to sweeten a recipe due to its naturally really sweet flavour. I choose to use date syrup rather than dates when I want the mixture to be completely smooth and when I need to add moisture. Date syrup can colour a mix quite significantly with a purple-like hue. If you want to retain a light colour in a recipe, maple syrup is often the better sweetener to use. I use Biona's date syrup.

COCONUT PALM SUGAR

HEALTH BENEFITS:

This sugar is derived from the flower buds of coconut trees. It has a minimal effect on blood sugar levels, making it a popular option for diabetics as well as amongst vegans and raw foodies. It provides a source of potassium, magnesium, zinc and iron, as well as vitamins B1, B2, B3 and B6. These B vitamins are important for nerve function, energy metabolism and protein metabolism.

HOW TO USE IT:

I use coconut palm sugar as a replacement for brown sugar in many recipes, such as some of my crumbles. It gives them sweetness with a hint of caramel similar in taste to brown sugar and it helps to intensify the flavour of other ingredients. I choose to use this sugar over a syrup when I don't want any other liquid to be put into a mix. I also tend to prefer to use this sugar for desserts rather than breakfasts, where I usually stick to using fruit. Coconut sugar is very sweet and is another ingredient where a little goes a long way.

AGAVE

I thought here would be an appropriate time to mention agave. Agave has had many mixed views presented in the media. Due to its property of being purely a 'fruit sugar', many people believe it to be healthy. The natural sugars found in fruits are healthier alternatives as they contain many vitamins, minerals and fibre. However, agave is purely the sugar, with none of the nutritional benefits and no fibre, which means that it is 90 per cent fructose. The liver struggles to digest this fructose due to the lack of fibre and it can become stored around the liver. For this reason, I choose not to use agave in my cooking.

SWEET SPICES – CINNAMON, VANILLA, ETC.

These sweet spices can effectively boost satiety and mimic sweetness, which allows us to cut back on sugar! Just 1 teaspoon of ground cinnamon packs in the same amount of antioxidants as a cup of fresh blueberries. Cinnamon is also a spice to note as it

stabilises blood sugar levels. By adding it to your breakfast in the morning, it can prevent cravings later on in the day.

Vanilla powder is an ingredient I use regularly to add a sweet hint of flavour to my recipes. Vanilla powder is a little more expensive and harder to find than essence, extract or paste. I prefer to use powder as it has no other ingredients, and is only the bean itself, while essence often contains sugar and ethanol. However, these alternatives can be used in the place of vanilla powder if preferred. Add these to taste as measurements have not been provided.

FRUIT

HEALTH BENEFITS:

When you consume fruit, you are not only consuming fructose (the fruit sugar in its natural state), but also a great amount of fibre and lots of vitamins, minerals and antioxidants.

HOW TO USE THEM:

Fresh fruit purées are great to use in baking as they provide good structural properties that help to bind ingredients. Apple purée is so easy to make and can also be bought without any preservatives, so it is a great ingredient to always have in your store cupboard.

To make apple purée, simply peel and core the apples (you can use any variety), and cut the flesh into small chunks. Transfer to a saucepan, add a little water and cook over a medium heat for approximately 20 minutes until soft. Once cooked, use a hand blender to make the apple into a purée.

Apple purée adds a hint of sweetness and is not too overpowering with its apple taste. I also use apple purée to add moisture to a mix. Biona have a totally natural apple purée, which is great to use in baking recipes.

I often use dried fruit in my cooking, first ensuring the fruit is the only ingredient as many store-bought products contain other ingredients. Dried fruit is good when you want to add a little extra chewiness to a recipe and also to help bind ingredients together.

BANANAS

HEALTH BENEFITS:

Bananas are naturally fat- and cholesterol-free, easy to digest and they make an amazing snack when you need a boost in energy. They are packed with potassium and are naturally low in sodium, which is the perfect combination to help maintain a healthy balance of fluids in the body, protect our cardiovascular system and keep blood pressure under control. The potassium in bananas is also good to prevent cramps after exercising due to its role in acid-base balance. The vitamin B6 present in bananas can help with sleep and the magnesium can help the muscles relax. Like most fruit, the amount of fibre helps keep the body regular, as well as curbing hunger and keeping us fuller for longer when combined with another protein snack.

HOW TO USE THEM:

I use bananas as a replacement for butter when needing a binder, and sugar when wanting something to be made naturally sweet. Bananas are wonderfully sweet and creamy and they are such a versatile ingredient to use in baking. I tend to use overly ripe bananas when I want to create a flavour with a strong banana taste and extra sweetness. Unripe bananas are better to use when they are needed for their functionality rather than for their taste. Blended or mashed bananas can act as a great binder and will provide a creamy moisture to the mix. I love using bananas in breakfast recipes, too, especially due to their many health benefits.

Equipment I use

FOOD PROCESSOR

The main piece of equipment that I use is a food processor. In most of my recipes a food processor is crucial. In order to make your own nut butters, flours, pie crusts, etc., a food processor with considerable power is essential. I have broken several mini processors in my time when trying to grind too many nuts at once, so do be cautious before loading your machine up too much.

Magimix is my favourite brand. I use the 5200XL, which is top of the range. For the amount of cooking and baking I do, this is quite essential. However, a smaller food processor may be preferable for many of you and this is absolutely fine. Just make sure that the blades you use are sharp enough as some of my recipes require the grinding down of nuts and other grains. A poor-quality food processor may struggle with breaking down tough food. If you are interested in this way of cooking, I would suggest that a good food processor goes on to the top of your wish list!

BROWNIE TINS AND DEEP BAKING TRAYS

For many of my recipes, including brownies, slabs and crumble squares, I use a brownie tin or a deep baking tray. The most common sizes I use are 20cm x 20cm square or a 20cm x 28cm rectangle. For tartlets, I also use mini dishes which have loose bottoms.

CAKE TINS

I use a number of different-sized cake tins, but most commonly 18cm in diameter. I tend to use a non-stick tin with quick-release clasps and a loose bottom for ease.

PIE AND TART TINS/DISHES

Although pies and tarts are not essentially the same thing, I tend to use the same dish for both. This is mainly because I like to use a loose-bottomed dish which is most common in a tart dish. A loose-bottomed tin makes getting the tart/pie out once made a lot easier! I use a 24cm round tart dish.

MUFFIN MOULDS

I use silicone muffin moulds simply due to the ease of getting the muffins out of them. Metal tins can often make the removal of the muffin a little trickier.

Online resources

If you don't live in a large city like London, it can be hard to get hold of certain ingredients. Here I have included a list of great online resources for buying the ingredients included in this book.

AMAZON

This online platform is amazing for groceries. When you lead a really busy life as I do, sometimes finding the time to get to a supermarket is hard. Amazon allows you to shop from home with such ease and they offer such a wide range of food. Pretty much every ingredient used in this book can be bought from Amazon, and they very often offer deals on bulk purchases, so when ordering multiple bags or tubs of something, I would highly recommend buying them here. It is great for items such as coconut oil, oat flour and date syrup.

OCADO

Ocado is my favourite online supermarket. The fact that you can choose the hour slot to receive your order is so convenient and makes life so easy. I do an Ocado shop twice a week and because of this I rarely need to go out to a shop! Ocado are amazing for fresh produce, and they also stock many of the healthy food brands so that you can buy raw chocolate, dates, quinoa and buckwheat flour from there, too. Fingers crossed you will also be able to buy Livia's Kitchen products from there one day!

REALFOODS.CO.UK & SUPERNUTRIENTS.CO.UK

These are fantastic online shops where you can buy superfood powders and other health products such as coconut sugar and coconut oil. They offer great discounts for bulk orders so for those who love products such as raw cacao powder as much as I do, it is definitely worth buying from one of these.

Staple Recipes

Milks

Being intolerant to dairy, I had to find an alternative to milk so that I could make all the baked goods I wanted. When I cut out dairy, one of the first things I did was visit the supermarket to have a look at the range of nut milks. But when I looked at their ingredient lists, I saw that most of them are just full of additives. Many nut milks found on supermarket shelves only contain around 2 per cent nuts, while a whole host of other ingredients are used to make up the remaining 98 per cent. Since most of the additives in processed foods make me really unwell, I set out to make my own home-made milk.

ALMOND MILK

I love the natural sweetness of almond milk, which allows you to use a little less sweetener in recipes. Almond milk in porridge, coffee and in baking is also such a great alternative if you are unable to tolerate dairy. It is a little less creamy than oat milk and so this should be considered when choosing which one to use in a baking recipe.

Makes Roughly 500ml Milk

350g blanched almonds, soaked for at least 6 hours in water
60g soft pitted Medjool dates
½ tsp vanilla powder

Drain and rinse the almonds. Blend the almonds, dates and 600–800ml water (depending on how thick you want the milk to be) in a food processor for about 5 minutes until the milk is fairly smooth.

Strain through a nut milk bag, ensuring you squeeze as much of the liquid out as possible.

Stir in the vanilla powder and store in a glass milk bottle with an airtight lid. Keep refrigerated and shake before use.

OAT MILK
{Nut Free}

Although I have conquered the art of making a great almond milk, oat milk for me is still the one! Firstly, it is so much cheaper than nut milk, secondly, it is so much easier to make, and thirdly, it gives a really amazing creamy texture to recipes without adding a very distinctive taste. What's more, making your own oat milk has a huge advantage over nut milks because no electric equipment is needed. None at all!

Makes Roughly 550ml Milk

100g rolled oats

Place the rolled oats in a bowl and leave to soak in 500ml cold or room-temperature water for 15 minutes.

Place a sieve over a second bowl and pour the soaked oats and water through the sieve.

Using a spoon, stir the oats in the sieve to make sure you are draining all the liquid from them. The oat milk will be collecting in the bowl under the sieve.

Once all the liquid is drained from the oats, place the soaked oats back into the first bowl and cover with 200ml cold or room-temperature water.

Leave the oats to soak for another 10 minutes, then repeat the above process, draining all the oat milk from the soaked oats into the second bowl.

Pour the oat milk into a glass milk bottle, screw on an airtight lid and store in the fridge. Shake well before using.

Nut Butters

Peanut butter has been a popular spread for many years, but now other nut butters are becoming much more accessible.

While home-made nut butters are made by simply dry roasting and then grinding the nuts for a few minutes, in many store-bought nut butters the roasted nuts are mixed with other ingredients such as sugar, salt, oils and emulsifiers. Check the ingredients to find ones that only contain nuts. Meridian offer many pure and natural nut butters and this is the brand I tend to use when I don't make my own.

Nut butters have become one of my most commonly used ingredients in baking (as well as being something I love to enjoy teaspoon after teaspoon by itself!). They can be used as a substitute for butter in many recipes, providing fat (the good fat found in nuts) and to help to bind a mix.

BLANCHED ALMOND VANILLA BUTTER

I prefer blanched almond butter to almond butter made with the skins on as it is slightly more sweet and less bitter. It also prevents a mixture from turning brown when you use it in a recipe. This is amazing to use as a spread and in baking, as well as being completely addictive when stuffed inside pitted dates for a little snack.

Makes 350g Butter

370g blanched almonds
1–2 teaspoons vanilla powder
1 tablespoon maple syrup

Roast the almonds for 10–12 minutes at 180°C/350°F/ Gas mark 4.

Blend the roasted almonds and vanilla powder in a food processor until you have a butter.

Add the maple syrup at the end and blitz for a few more seconds, being careful not to over process.

Keep in an airtight jar.

PECAN & MACA BUTTER

Pecan butter is one of my favourite snacks. I only discovered how much
I loved this type of nut butter and how amazing and versatile it can be when
I made it for my Pecan Pie (page 139) filling.

Makes Roughly 400g Butter

260g pecans

150ml maple syrup

2 tablespoons maca powder

1 tablespoon ground cinnamon

Put all the ingredients in a food processor and mix for about 5 minutes
until completely smooth and there are no pecan pieces left.

Keep in an airtight jar.

THE ULTIMATE PASTRY

{ Nut Free }

Although this may be one of the most simple recipes in the book, it might just be the one of which I am most proud. I never thought it would be possible to create a pastry that tastes this good without, the use of wheat, flour and butter. This recipe is one I absolutely could not live without since it has given me the flexibility to make so many exciting creations. The pastry works best with shop-bought oat flour or ground jumbo oats that have been sifted. Fine oatmeal can work, but not as well.

Makes Enough for a 24cm Pie Base

35g raw coconut oil, plus
    extra softened coconut oil
    for greasing the dish
200g oat flour
90ml maple syrup
generous pinch of vanilla
    powder, ground
    cinnamon or ground
    ginger (optional)

TO MAKE THE CRUST

Melt the coconut oil so that it is liquid. Leave to cool for a few minutes after melting.

Combine all the ingredients in a large bowl and stir with a spoon until well mixed.

Knead with your hands to allow them to come together, making sure your hands are not too warm as this may cause the pastry to crumble a little.

To make a pastry base, lay a large piece of cling film on your kitchen counter or table. Position the ball of pastry in the middle of the cling film. Cover the top of the ball with another large piece of film and roll the pastry between the two sheets using a rolling pin.

TO LINE A TIN

Place the mix in a greased pie dish and, with your hand, flatten it out across the base and the sides. Make sure it is evenly spread across the dish.

TO COOK THE CRUST

Preheat the oven to 180°C/350°F/Gas mark 4.

Bake the crust in the oven for 10–15 minutes until the sides are slightly golden.

STICKY NUT CRUST

This pastry is one that can be used time and time again. It is the most simple and quickest of the pie crusts in this book and is so special because it only consists of five ingredients. It can be eaten raw or baked; for a slightly chewier crust, it should be left raw, but when looking for a crispier version, bake it in the oven.

Makes Enough for a 24cm Pie Base

small amount of softened
  coconut oil, for greasing
  the dish
130g pecans
155g almonds
165g soft pitted Medjool dates
¼ teaspoon salt

TO MAKE THE CRUST

Grease a pie dish with the coconut oil.

With a food processor, crush the nuts with the dates and salt until the nuts are in very small pieces and the dates make the mixture gooey. Use your hands to check the stickiness of the mix. It should all bind together well. If not, then use a few extra dates and pulse the mix again.

TO LINE A TIN

Place the mix in the pie dish and, with your hand, flatten it out across the base and the sides. Make sure it is evenly spread across the dish.

The crust can either be eaten raw or cooked.

FOR A COOKED CRUST

Preheat the oven to 180°C/350°F/Gas mark 4.

Bake the crust in the oven for 10–15 minutes until the sides are browning.

QUINOA & DATE CRUST

{Nut Free}

I was very keen to create an alternative pie crust that does not require either nuts or oats. This option works perfectly either raw or baked and takes absolutely no time at all to make. This crust will allow you to still really taste the filling of the pie or tart you are making, since it is not overpowering in flavour.

Makes Enough for a 24cm Pie Base

70g quinoa pops

220g soft pitted Medjool dates

1 tablespoon softened raw coconut oil, plus extra softened coconut oil for greasing the dish

generous pinch of vanilla powder, ground cinnamon or ground ginger (optional)

TO MAKE THE CRUST

Blend everything in a food processor until it is sticky and comes together.

TO LINE A TIN

Grease a 24cm pie dish. Place the mix in the dish and, with your hand, flatten it out across the base and the sides. Make sure it is evenly spread across the dish.

FOR A COOKED CRUST

Preheat the oven to 180°C/350°F/Gas mark 4.

Bake the crust in the oven for 15–20 minutes until the sides are browning.

SWEET DATE & CASHEW BUTTER FROSTING

This frosting is creamy and easy to spread, so is great on cakes and biscuits. Meridian do a really lovely smooth cashew butter and I tend to use that when making this recipe. It also works really well with a hint of coffee, so you can just choose whether you add instant coffee to it or not.

Makes Roughly 250g Frosting

3–4 teaspoons instant coffee (optional)
40ml boiling water
175g cashew butter
50ml date syrup
½ teaspoon vanilla powder

Add the coffee powder to the boiling water, if using.

Stir all the ingredients together in a bowl and spoon onto a cake or a slice once cooled.

CINNAMON CASHEW CREAM

A cream is sometimes an essential part of a dessert and it can add moisture and a smooth texture to a cake or pudding. Although this is not 'cream' as you may know it (it's made from nuts as opposed to dairy), this version serves the same purpose, and in my opinion is much more delicious. It is slightly denser than your average cream, so not as much is needed, while the cinnamon and vanilla provide a natural sweetness.

Makes Roughly 750g Cream

500g cashews
2 teaspoons vanilla powder
4 teaspoons ground cinnamon
80ml maple syrup

Soak the cashews overnight or for a minimum of 4–6 hours. Drain and rinse.

Whizz the soaked nuts in a food processor or blender along with 80ml water until pretty much smooth.

Add all the other ingredients and whizz until totally smooth and creamy.

DARK CHOCOLATE
{Nut Free}

It amazes me how easy it is to make your own chocolate, I had no idea.
I really missed out for the first 25 years of my life! This recipe works
time and time again, and just goes to show how delicious natural
chocolate can be without the ingredients that are commonly found in
shop-bought chocolate.

Makes Roughly 175g Chocolate

65g cacao butter
40g cacao powder
4 tablespoons maple syrup
½ teaspoon vanilla powder
pinch of salt

Melt the cacao butter in a bain-marie or a glass bowl sitting above, but not
touching, a small saucepan of simmering water.

Add the other ingredients and stir until you have a smooth chocolate.

For slabs of dark chocolate, pour the mix into a mould and set in the fridge
for at least 2 hours. Dark chocolate can be kept in the fridge or left at room
temperature.

This dark chocolate recipe can also be used to cover biscuits and other treats.
Pour the chocolate over the biscuits or dip them into the bowl of chocolate to
cover them. Lay the biscuits out on a tray lined with greaseproof paper and set
in the fridge for 2 hours.

LEMON FROSTING

This is so wonderfully tangy and citrussy and has such a bright colour to it
that it makes any cake look so pretty!

Makes Roughly 390g Frosting

2 avocados
juice of 2½ lemons
zest of 1½ lemons
4½ tablespoons maple syrup
3 tablespoons almond butter (store-bought works best here as it is slightly runnier)

Mix all the ingredients together in a food processor until the mixture is
smooth and creamy and no pieces of avocado are visible. Spoon onto a
cake or a slice.

CHOCOLATE AVOCADO FROSTING

This is one of the recipes in the book that I use multiple times. It took me a little while to develop it. Trying to create a rich and creamy frosting that set well was a little challenging, but that made it even more exciting when it was achieved. You would never believe there was avocado in it, so don't be scared by it! The avocado makes this wonderfully creamy and nutritious, and the cacao makes it perfectly chocolatey.

Makes Roughly 325g Frosting

1 ripe avocado
5 tablespoons maple syrup
4 tablespoons cacao powder
3 tablespoons almond butter (store-bought works best here as it is slightly runnier)
2 tablespoons softened raw coconut oil

Blend all the ingredients together in a food processor until the mixture is glossy, creamy and completely combined.

Spoon on to a cooled cake or a slice.

STRABERRY JAM
{*Nut Free*}

I can guarantee that you will never want to go back to shop-bought jam after you make this recipe. It is surprisingly simple – there are just three ingredients and it is exactly what you are looking for in a jam, but without the refined sugars. You can store this in the fridge in an airtight container for a few weeks. Perfect for toast and as an ingredient in baking recipes.

Makes Roughly 750g Jam
750g strawberries, hulled and chopped
35g white chia seeds
60g coconut palm sugar

Add everything to a large pan with 100ml water and cook over a medium heat for 15–20 minutes, stirring occasionally, until the mix becomes thick with a jelly-like consistency. It will begin to thicken even more as it cools.

Pour into an airtight jar when totally cool and store in the fridge.

FIG JAM

{Nut Free}

This is a slightly more unusual-flavoured jam, and a little less sweet than the strawberry one. For those of you who like a really sweet jam, a few more tablespoons of coconut sugar can be added, but I personally love the option of having a little less sweetness.

Makes Roughly 460g Jam

350g figs (roughly 8), chopped into small pieces
¼ teaspoon ground cinnamon
¼ teaspoon vanilla powder
4 tablespoons coconut palm sugar
30g white chia seeds

Add everything to a large pan with 100ml water and bubble for 15–20 minutes, stirring occasionally, until thick with a jelly-like consistency. It will thicken even more as it cools.

Pour into an airtight jar when totally cool and store in the fridge.

DATE CARAMEL

{Nut Free}

In so many conventional baking recipes, a sticky, caramel-like mix is commonly needed, so it was essential that I came up with one to use in my recipes. By adding just one ingredient to this recipe you can really make a big change to it, which is why I've suggested a number of variations. This is also great as a spread and a frosting.

Makes Roughly 365g Caramel

350g pitted soft Medjool dates

¼ teaspoon salt

3 tablespoons softened raw coconut oil

Add all the ingredients to a food processor.

Blitz until the mixture is thick and sticky and there are no visible dates.

Variations

ORANGE CARAMEL *{Nut Free}*

300ml fresh orange juice

2 tablespoons orange zest

The sweetness of the dates mixed with the citrus of the oranges makes such a perfect flavour.

PEANUT BUTTER CARAMEL

6 tablespoons smooth or crunchy peanut butter

For all peanut butter fans, this should be your go-to staple. By mixing peanut butter into the Date Caramel you create a subtle nutty flavour, which is amazing to add to certain cakes and biscuits.

COFFEE CARAMEL *{Nut Free}*

2 tablespoons instant coffee dissolved in 1 tablespoon boiling water

By adding coffee, which is quite bitter, to the sweet Date Caramel you get such an interesting and deep flavour. All coffee fans will love this. This frosting works so well on anything chocolatey!

Breakfast

RAW FRUITY GRANOLA BARS

{*Nut Free*}

These make such a refreshing change to the granola bars that are shop-bought and generally filled with many additives and preservatives. These bars take about 2 minutes to make and can be kept fresh for weeks. They are the ultimate on-the-go breakfast, designed to keep you full from lots of good-for-you ingredients.

Makes 10–12 bars

200g jumbo oats
50g sunflower seeds
125g soft pitted Medjool dates
60g prunes
70g raisins
60g apple purée or unsweetened apple sauce
75g buckwheat groats
1 teaspoon ground cinnamon
a sprinkle of salt

Place all the ingredients in a food processor and blitz until the mixture is sticky and well combined.

Place the granola in a 20cm x 20cm brownie tin and spread it out evenly until it is about 1cm thick. Cut into bar shapes with a knife.

Store in the fridge if a firmer texture is preferred. The bars can also be kept at room temperature in an airtight container.

BAKED CINNAMON
& BANANA BARS

{Nut Free}

Hot out of the oven, these bars make one of the most comforting breakfast options ever! Although I love them freshly baked, they are also really good when kept in an airtight container and used as a grab-and-go breakfast when time is limited. The cinnamon gives the banana a deep, rich flavour and extra natural sweetness.

Makes 8–10 Bars

220g soft pitted Medjool dates
2½ tablespoons ground cinnamon
sprinkle of salt
150g ripe peeled bananas
50g melted raw coconut oil
200g jumbo oats

Preheat the oven to 180°C/350°F/Gas mark 4.

Mix the dates, cinnamon, salt, bananas and coconut oil in a food processor until well mixed and sticky.

Stir in the oats until well mixed together.

Evenly spread the mixture in a 20cm x 20cm brownie tin so that it is about 2cm thick.

Bake for 15 minutes until they start to brown on top.

The bars should be kept at room temperature in an airtight container.

RAW MATCHA
GRANOLA BARS
{Nut Free}

I am a newly converted matcha fan. When choosing what type of tea my early morning cup will be, I sometimes have a bit of a dilemma. I do also love English breakfast tea and so often choose this over matcha. To help with my morning tea predicament, I came up with the idea of incorporating matcha into a breakfast granola bar that I could eat whilst sipping on my cup of English breakfast tea. Best of both worlds!

Makes 10–12 Bars

120g jumbo oats

50g pumpkin seeds

150g prunes

100g raisins

50g finely desiccated coconut

1 tablespoon matcha powder

pinch of salt

Put all the ingredients in a food processor and blitz until the mixture is sticky and well combined.

Place the mixture into a 20cm x 20cm brownie tin and spread it out evenly to about 1cm thick.

Cut into bar shapes with a knife and put in the fridge.

Store in the fridge if a firmer texture is preferred. The bars can also be kept at room temperature in an airtight container.

RAW MOCHA GRANOLA BARS

I never really was a coffee person, but I love to use it in a variety of different ways in baking. These granola bars are filling and have a subtle taste of both chocolate and coffee. They are the perfect morning snack, but I also love them in the afternoons as a little pick-me-up. The buckwheat groats in this recipe give the bars a really unusual texture and crunch, which I love!

Makes 10–12 Bars

100g jumbo oats
200g soft pitted Medjool dates
100g raisins
75g buckwheat groats
2 tablespoons instant coffee dissolved in 3 tablespoons boiling water
2 tablespoons cacao powder
2 tablespoons almond butter (optional)

Mix all the ingredients in a food processor until well combined and sticky.

Flatten the mixture into a 20cm x 20cm brownie tin until even and about 1cm thick.

Cut into bar shapes with a knife.

Store in the fridge if a firmer texture is preferred. The bars can also be kept at room temperature in an airtight container.

Porridge Muffins and Squares

When there is no time for a hot bowl of porridge, a porridge muffin or square is the next best thing. These make such good, filling breakfasts and are suitable for those of you who are nut free.

APPLE & RAISIN SPROUTED PORRIDGE MUFFINS

{Nut Free}

This muffin recipe uses sprouted oats, which add a really interesting flavour and are also easier to digest than other oats. Normal oats can be used as a substitute and the muffins will still be great.

Makes 12 Muffins

softened coconut oil, for
   greasing the tins
260g sprouted oats
400ml Oat Milk (page 44)
3 Granny Smith apples
120g oat flour
2 tablespoons maple syrup
230g raisins
3 teaspoons ground cinnamon
1½ teaspoons ground ginger
sprinkle of nutmeg
pinch of salt

Preheat the oven to 180°C/350°F/Gas mark 4.

Grease one or two muffin tins with the coconut oil or line with muffin paper cases.

Pour the sprouted oats and oat milk into a mixing bowl to soak whilst you peel and grate the apples.

Add the grated apple, flour, maple syrup, raisins, cinnamon, ginger, nutmeg and salt into the mixing bowl with the oats and oat milk. Mix together.

Spoon the mixture into the muffin tins.

Place in the oven and bake for 20 minutes until the muffins start to brown on top. They should feel bouncy when first out of the oven, but firm up when cool.

BLUEBERRY PORRIDGE SQUARES

{Nut Free}

Blueberries in the morning are hard to beat. And when used in recipes, other ingredients are almost superfluous as blueberries provide an amazing taste that you don't want to mask. This is one of the most popular recipes on my blog.

Makes 12 Big Squares

300g jumbo oats
225g blueberries, plus an extra 60g to stir through
225ml Oat Milk (page 44)
½ teaspoon vanilla powder
115ml maple syrup

Preheat the oven to 180°C/350°F/Gas mark 4.

Line a 20cm x 20cm brownie tin with greaseproof paper.

Add all the ingredients to a blender or food processor except for the 60g of blueberries and pulse until combined.

Stir through the extra blueberries.

Pour the mixture into the lined tin and bake in the oven for 15 minutes until the squares are firm, but still bouncy. Make sure the middle is cooked – it may need an extra few minutes.

Leave to cool and then slice into squares.

Pancakes

I love to make pancakes at the weekend when there is a little more time. Topped with maple syrup or coconut yoghurt and fruit, these are just the absolute best to serve for brunch. Although commonly made with wheat flour and milk, pancakes can be made in a variety of different ways and I have had such fun experimenting with them. These are my three favourite pancake recipes.

CACAO & HAZELNUT PANCAKES

I used to be a huge Nutella fan and had it on everything, especially pancakes. So when coming up with recipes for pancakes, I thought why not use the same ingredients and flavour combination as those used in Nutella to make up the pancake rather than spreading it on them?!

Makes 8 Pancakes

300g ripe peeled bananas
300ml Oat Milk (page 44)
120g hazelnut butter
125g rolled oats
¼ teaspoon salt
20g cacao powder
coconut oil, for greasing the pan

Mix all the ingredients using a food processor or an electric whisk until well combined.

Heat a frying pan and melt some coconut oil.

Using a ladle, spoon out one ladle of the mixture per pancake and cook the pancakes until they begin to brown on each side.

BLUEBERRY & BANANA OAT PANCAKES

{ Nut Free }

Whenever I go for fruit in the mornings, it will either be blueberries or bananas. I absolutely love to use them in breakfast recipes, and combined they complement each other perfectly. The flavour of each fruit comes through strongly in these pancakes, especially with a little maple syrup and some extra bananas on top.

Makes 8 Pancakes

160g oat flour
240g very ripe peeled bananas
400ml Oat Milk (page 44)
pinch of salt
220g blueberries
coconut oil, for greasing the pan

Mix all the ingredients together with 150g of the blueberries using a food processor or an electric whisk until well blended, but with the blueberries still in small pieces.

Stir in the remaining unblended blueberries.

Heat a frying pan and melt some coconut oil.

Using a ladle, spoon out one ladle of the mixture per pancake and cook the pancakes until they begin to brown on each side.

ALMOND &
MACA PANCAKES

These are simply scrumptious and a perfect no-grain recipe. The
maca gives the pancakes a unique caramel taste and offers great
nutritional value.

Makes 5–6 Pancakes

200ml Almond Milk (page 42)
80g buckwheat flour
25ml maple syrup, plus extra for serving
2½ tablespoons maca powder
pinch of salt
2 tablespoons almond butter (store-bought works best here as it is slightly runnier)
coconut oil, for greasing the pan
sliced banana, for serving
chopped almonds, for serving

Mix all the ingredients using a food processor or an electric whisk until
well combined.

Heat a frying pan and melt some coconut oil.

Using a ladle, spoon out one ladle of the mixture per pancake and cook the
pancakes until they begin to brown on each side.

Serve with sliced banana, chopped almonds and a drizzle of maple syrup.

Breakfast Oat Balls

These are just perfect to make the night before a busy day, when you know you won't have time to prepare breakfast in the morning. A couple of these provide so much goodness and keep you going for hours. They are so simple, tasty and satisfying. Make them whatever size you like – I personally love making them quite small and taking a handful as my breakfast or as a mid-morning snack.

APPLE & CINNAMON OAT BALLS

{Nut Free}

The apple and cinnamon flavour combination has always been a favourite of mine, so I have used these ingredients to make these incredibly simple and satisfying breakfast balls.

Makes about 12–15 Balls

200g grated apple
150g soft pitted Medjool dates
¾ teaspoon ground cinnamon
40g flaxseed
20g white chia seeds
200g jumbo oats

Mix all the ingredients except the oats in a food processor until well combined.

Stir in the jumbo oats.

Roll into balls using your hands.

Store in the fridge in an airtight container to keep fresh for longer.

COFFEE SHOT BREAKFAST BALLS

This recipe is for all of you who love your coffee in the morning. I thought the idea of putting a coffee shot into a breakfast oat ball was such a fun idea. This coffee shot ball allows you to kill two birds with one stone; eat your breakfast and have your coffee all at the same time.

Makes about 10–12 Balls

200g jumbo oats or blanched almonds

40g flaxseed

3 tablespoons instant coffee dissolved in 2 tablespoons boiling water

100g raisins

150g soft pitted Medjool dates

5 tablespoons almond butter (store-bought works best here as it is slightly runnier)

30g white chia seeds

Blend all the ingredients except for the chia seeds in a food processor until well mixed.

Roll the mixture into balls.

Roll the balls in a bowl of the chia seeds until they are evenly coated.

Store in the fridge in an airtight container to keep fresh for longer.

CARROT OAT BALLS

{Nut Free}

Carrots provide a perfectly subtle sweetness to a recipe. I was always given carrots to snack on when I was little, and they remain one of my favourite snacks. Carrots are a rich source of antioxidants and vitamins, and so I like to get them in wherever I can! This recipe is essentially a simplified carrot cake recipe but much less sweet. This makes them a wonderful breakfast option, and I love them as a snack throughout the day, too.

Makes about 12–15 Balls

200g grated carrot
180g soft pitted Medjool dates
¼ teaspoon ground cinnamon
¼ teaspoon ground nutmeg
25g flaxseed
10g white chia seeds
125g jumbo oats

Mix all the ingredients except the oats in a food processor
until well combined.

Stir in the jumbo oats.

Roll into balls using your hands.

Store in the fridge in an airtight container to keep fresh for longer.

BANANA BREAD
{Nut Free}

Although this is essentially a cake, I love to eat it in the mornings with nut butter spread and sliced banana on top. A slice of this is perfectly filling and keeps you sated until lunch. Of course, it also makes a great afternoon snack.

Makes 1 Loaf

softened coconut oil, for greasing the tin
550g ripe peeled bananas, plus extra sliced for serving
75g rolled oats, or chopped blanched almonds if the recipe does not need to be nut free
150g oat flour or almond flour
½ teaspoon ground cinnamon
100ml maple syrup

Preheat the oven to 180°C/350°F/Gas mark 4.

Grease a 20cm x 11cm loaf tin with coconut oil or line with greaseproof paper.

Mix all the ingredients together in a bowl with your hands or an electric mixer.

Pour the mixture into the loaf tin and bake for 45 minutes.

This is best stored in an airtight container in the fridge to help it stay fresh for longer.

BANANA & CACAO
QUINOA BOWL

{ Nut Free }

This is something a little different. It could perhaps be classed as a porridge, but a very unique one! The bananas in this recipe act as a natural sweetener, but also as a creamy substance that binds the cooked quinoa. With the added cacao, there is a rich chocolatey flavour that every chocolate fan will die for! This recipe is so divine hot or cold, and is definitely going to be one for kids.

Makes 4–5 Breakfast Bowls

120g uncooked quinoa
300g ripe peeled bananas, mashed or chopped
20g cacao powder
30g date syrup
50g finely desiccated coconut
pinch of salt
coconut flakes, seeds or chopped banana, for toppings

Cook the quinoa as per the cooking instructions. Remove from the heat once cooked and the water has been absorbed.

Add all the other ingredients into the quinoa and stir well.

The quinoa bowl can be served hot or cold with a topping of coconut flakes, seeds or chopped banana.

Any extra can be stored in an airtight container in the fridge for a few days.

Flapjacks, Brownies and Squares

PEANUT BUTTER & JELLY CAKE SQUARES

When I was little I used to love peanut butter and jelly (strawberry jam) sandwiches. Here I have taken the concept and made it into a ridiculously irresistible blondie. By using my staple strawberry jam recipe and spreading it on top of the peanut butter blondie, you combine two simple recipes that truly complement each other.

Makes 12–15 Squares

300g peanut butter
150ml maple syrup
150g buckwheat flour
200g ripe peeled bananas, mashed
½ Strawberry Jam recipe (page 58)

Preheat the oven to 180°C/350°F/Gas mark 4.

Line a 20cm x 28cm brownie tin with greaseproof paper.

Mix all the ingredients except for the jam in a bowl and then spoon into the tin.

Spread the jam on top.

Bake for 20 minutes and then leave to cool before slicing.

RAW MATCHA & CHOCOLATE SLAB

As a newly converted matcha green tea fan and, obviously (looking at my recipes), a massive chocolate fan too, it made sense to combine these flavours to create something so unbelievably moreish. The texture of the nutty matcha base combined with the smooth chocolate avocado frosting is perfect.

Makes 12–15 Squares

BASE

140g raw or blanched almonds
40g buckwheat groats
270g soft pitted Medjool dates
10g matcha powder
50g finely desiccated coconut
sprinkle of salt

Chocolate Avocado Frosting (page 57), with 1 tablespoon matcha powder added
2 tablespoons raw coconut chips or desiccated coconut, to decorate
1–2 tablespoons cacao nibs, to decorate

TO MAKE THE BASE

Blend all the base ingredients together until well mixed and a sticky consistency is achieved.

Line a 20cm x 20cm brownie tin with greaseproof paper. Push the mix evenly into the tin. The base should be about 1cm thick.

Cover the base with the frosting.

Place the slab in the fridge to allow the frosting to set. Slice just before serving. This slab is best served straight out of the fridge.

Sprinkle some coconut chips or desiccated coconut and the cacao nibs over the top before serving.

ALL (COCONUT) BUTTER FLAPJACKS

{ Nut Free }

At the secondary school I attended we were always given hot flapjacks at morning break. These were surely filled with butter and refined sugars, but my friends and I all loved them. I was dubious as to whether the same indulgent flavour and texture could be achieved without the golden syrup and butter, but this shows it very much can be.

Makes 12–15 Flapjacks

95g coconut butter
350g jumbo oats
110ml maple syrup
60ml date syrup
85g raw honey

Preheat the oven to 180°C/350°F/Gas mark 4.

Line a 20cm x 28cm brownie tin with greaseproof paper.

Melt the coconut butter by placing the glass jar in a bowl or pan of warm water.

Mix all the ingredients together in a bowl.

Spoon into the tin and smooth out the top.

Place into the oven for 15 minutes until the flapjacks start to slightly brown on top.

Cut into flapjacks and then leave to cool completely before lifting from the tray.

CHOCOLATE ORANGE AVOCADO BROWNIES

Avocado in sweet recipes was a total revelation for me. It can act as butter and provides a wonderful creamy texture. The cacao here masks the flavour of the avocado and these are everything you'd expect from a brownie: chocolatey, dense and slightly gooey at the same time.

Makes 12–15 Brownies

175ml maple syrup

250g buckwheat flour or almond flour

50g almond butter

¼ teaspoon salt

30g cacao powder

300ml orange juice and pulp

2 oranges

2 (350g) really ripe avocados

Preheat the oven to 180°C/350°F/Gas mark 4.

Line a 20cm x 28cm brownie tin with greaseproof paper.

Put the maple syrup, flour, almond butter, salt and cacao powder in a mixing bowl.

Squeeze the oranges using a hand-held squeezer, getting all the juice and a bit of pulp. Then pour into the mixing bowl.

Grate the outside of the oranges, collecting the zest so that you have 1 teaspoon in total, which can then be added to the mix.

Stone the avocados and spoon them out into the bowl.

Blitz together using an electric hand-held mixer.

Pour the mixture into the greased brownie tin and make sure the mix is evenly distributed across the tin.

Bake for 20–25 minutes until the mix has begun to firm up, but is still bouncy, making sure the middle is not wet before taking out of the oven.

Leave to cool for 10 minutes, then slice into squares and remove from the tin.

RAW ORANGE CARAMEL SLAB

My love of the chocolate orange combination comes through again here. With a chocolatey biscuit base, the sweet, sticky orange caramel and thin, crisp chocolate layer on top is pure delight.

Makes 12–15 Squares

BASE
75g rolled oats
50g buckwheat groats
3 tablespoons cacao powder
150g soft pitted Medjool dates
75g raisins
50g almond butter
sprinkle of salt

¾ Orange Caramel recipe (page 61)
Dark Chocolate (page 54)

TO MAKE THE BASE

Line a 20cm x 20cm brownie tin with greaseproof paper.

Mix all the ingredients for the base in a food processor and press this down into the base of the tin until you have an even layer.

Spoon the Orange Caramel mixture onto the base and leave to set in the freezer.

Pour the Dark Chocolate on top.

Leave in the freezer for at least 3 hours and preferably overnight.

Remove the slab from the freezer 10–15 minutes before slicing to prevent it from cracking. Keep stored in the fridge or freezer.

RAW CHUNKY PEANUT BUTTER SLAB

If you are a chocolate and peanut butter fan, then this is a must for you. This is one of the most popular recipes on my blog. When eaten together, the combination of the different delicious layers is a unique and addictive treat.

Makes 12–15 Squares

NOUGAT
125g rolled oats or oat flour (can also be replaced by more ground almonds)
125g ground almonds
30ml maple syrup
25g melted raw coconut oil
1½ teaspoons vanilla powder

PEANUT CARAMEL
350g soft pitted Medjool dates
¼ teaspoon salt
95g peanut butter
½ teaspoon vanilla powder
2 tablespoons melted raw coconut oil
40g peanuts (toasted preferably, or raw)

RAW CHOCOLATE
100g raw coconut oil
60g cacao powder
2 teaspoons vanilla powder
pinch of salt
4 tablespoons maple syrup

TO MAKE THE NOUGAT
If using whole rolled oats, place them in a food processor and grind to a flour-like consistency.

Add all the other ingredients and pulse until the mixture comes together.

Line a 20cm x 20cm brownie tin with greaseproof paper. Press the mix into the tin and place in the freezer while you make the peanut caramel filling.

TO MAKE THE PEANUT CARAMEL
Blend the dates until they form a paste and then add the other ingredients, except for the whole peanuts, blending until a smooth caramel forms.

Add the peanuts and pulse a few times so that they are combined with the caramel mixture.

Spread onto the base in the tin. Return to the freezer.

TO MAKE THE RAW CHOCOLATE
Melt the coconut oil in a bain-marie or a glass bowl sitting above, but not touching, a small saucepan of simmering water.

Once melted, add all the other ingredients and stir until you have a nice smooth chocolate.

Pour the chocolate onto the other two layers and leave to set in the freezer for at least an hour.

Remove the slab from the freezer 10–15 minutes before slicing to prevent it from cracking.

RAW CHRISTMAS FLAPJACKS

{ Nut Free }

When we were little, my mum started buying Christmassy treats at the beginning of the season and we were never without festive snacks. Although I can no longer eat many of these treats, I still want my home to always be full of Christmassy goodies and so I experimented with the flavours of Christmas to create some really simple flapjacks that would be ideal to have around the house.

Makes about 14 Flapjacks

200g jumbo oats

250g soft pitted Medjool dates

75g soft dried apricots

1 teaspoon ground cinnamon

½ teaspoon ground nutmeg

½ teaspoon ground allspice

¼ teaspoon ground ginger

20g flaxseed

pinch of salt

Mix all the ingredients in a food processor until well combined.

Spread into a 20cm x 28cm brownie tin and cut into stars for a festive twist or squares.

Store in airtight jars for 2–3 days.

RAW FROSTED CHOCOLATE BROWNIES

These were some of the first raw treats I ever made, and after seeing how simple to make and totally delicious they could be, there was no going back for me! These raw brownies are perfectly gooey and indulgent and contain such simple ingredients. The hazelnuts, like most other nuts, are rich in protein and essential fatty acids, and they give the brownie a 'Nutella' flavour.

Makes 12–15 Brownies

300g raw hazelnuts
300g soft pitted Medjool dates
5 tablespoons cacao powder
1 tablespoon maple syrup
¼ teaspoon salt

Chocolate Avocado Frosting
   (page 57)
2 tablespoons cacao powder,
   for dusting
1–2 tablespoons cacao nibs, to
   decorate (optional)

Whizz 200g of the raw hazelnuts in a food processor until a fine, flour-like substance is formed.

Add all the other brownie ingredients, except for the remaining hazelnuts. Process until the mixture is smooth, well mixed and sticky.

Add the remaining hazelnuts and process until the nuts have been broken down into small pieces. You want to be able to still see small pieces of nut.

Line a 20cm x 28cm brownie tin with greaseproof paper. Place the mixture into the tin and smooth the mix out across the tin so that it is about 1cm thick.

Top with the Chocolate Avocado Frosting.

Leave to set in the fridge for 20–30 minutes.

Sprinkle a light dusting of cacao powder and cacao nibs, if using, over the top before serving.

RAW BANOFFEE
PIE SLAB

Here is another take on a three-layered slab recipe. I use a softer chocolate for this rather than the staple dark chocolate. The three layers look amazing, but more importantly, they taste even better!

Makes about 12 Squares

NOUGAT
165g rolled oats or oat flour
    (can also be replaced by
    more ground almonds)
165g ground almonds
50ml maple syrup
25g melted raw coconut oil
1½ teaspoons vanilla powder

BANANA CARAMEL
350g soft pitted Medjool dates
150g very ripe peeled bananas

RAW CHOCOLATE
100g raw coconut oil
60g cacao powder
2 teaspoons vanilla powder
pinch of salt
4 tablespoons maple syrup

2 tablespoons cacao powder,
    for dusting
1 banana, sliced, to decorate

TO MAKE THE NOUGAT
If using whole rolled oats rather than flour, place the oats in a food processor and grind to a flour-like consistency.

Add all the other ingredients and pulse until the mixture comes together.

Line a 20cm x 28cm brownie tin with greaseproof paper. Press the mixture into the tin and place in the freezer while you make the banana caramel.

TO MAKE THE BANANA CARAMEL
Blend the dates until they form a paste. Add the banana, blending until a smooth caramel forms.

Spread onto the base in the tin and then return it to the freezer.

TO MAKE THE RAW CHOCOLATE
Melt the coconut oil in a bain-marie or a glass bowl above, not touching, a pan of simmering water.

Once melted, add all the other ingredients and stir until you have a nice smooth chocolate.

Pour the chocolate onto the other two layers and leave to set in the freezer for at least an hour.

Remove the banoffee slice from the freezer at least 10 minutes before slicing to prevent it from cracking. Dust with cacao powder and serve with banana slices on top.

Crumble Squares

As I mentioned in the introduction, the product that kicked off my business and which was introduced into stores was crumble. Crumble is a quintessentially British pudding and for as long as I can remember has been my number one dessert. The combination of fresh fruit compote with a sumptuous crumble topping cannot be beaten.

Since I slightly shook up the traditional recipe by giving it a nutritional and superfood twist, I thought for the book I should shake it up even more. Instead of just creating more crumble recipes served in the conventional way and eaten with a spoon, I have designed some recipes for squares that can be bitten into like a flapjack. With fruit compote sandwiched between a biscuit base and topping, you are able to enjoy the whole experience of crumble in a totally different way.

NECTARINE & COCONUT CRUMBLE SQUARES

Nectarine crumble isn't the most traditional flavour, but it really should be! These crumble squares are incredibly fruity, moreish and comforting.

Makes 12 Squares

NECTARINE FILLING

2 nectarines, stoned and
  chopped into chunks
35g coconut palm sugar
40g finely desiccated coconut
35ml boiling water

CRUMBLE

145g jumbo oats, plus 50g
  for the topping
65g pecans
15g finely desiccated coconut
150g pitted Medjool dates
55g melted raw coconut oil
1 tablespoon coconut palm
  sugar
pinch of salt

2 tablespoons raw coconut
  chips or desiccated coconut,
  to decorate

Preheat the oven to 180°C/350°F/Gas mark 4.

Line a 20cm x 20cm brownie tin with greaseproof paper.

TO MAKE THE NECTARINE FILLING

Put the chopped nectarines in a saucepan with the coconut palm sugar and desiccated coconut. Measure out the boiling water and add to the saucepan. Bring all the ingredients to the boil, stir and cook over a high heat for 5 minutes until the fruit is soft but not broken down.

TO MAKE THE CRUMBLE

Put the 145g of oats and the pecans in a food processor and grind until they form a fine flour-like mixture.

Add all the other ingredients except the remaining oats to the blender and blend until the mixture is sticky.

Using two-thirds of the crumble mix, make a base layer in the brownie tin, about 1cm deep. Spoon the nectarine mixture on top and spread evenly.

To the remaining crumble mix, add the rest of the oats and sprinkle this on top of the nectarines.

Bake in the oven for 10 minutes until the crumble topping starts to brown slightly.

Leave to cool completely, sprinkle with coconut and slice into squares.

APPLE CRUMBLE SQUARES

Here I have made the most traditional crumble flavour into a crumble square. My very special friend, Alyssia, was spending time with me whilst I created this recipe. She was my taster for the day, and she really helped me perfect the recipe. Not only did she assist me with this, but she has been invaluably supportive of everything I have done, and so I dedicate this recipe to her.

Makes 12 Squares

CRUMBLE

70g raisins
175g raw or blanched almonds
¼ teaspoon salt
½ teaspoon ground cinnamon
1 tablespoon firm raw coconut oil
110g pitted prunes
1 tablespoon coconut palm sugar
100g buckwheat flakes (oats
    could be used instead)

APPLE FILLING

4 large Granny Smith apples,
    peeled and chopped into pieces
    (about 400g once chopped)
1 tablespoon coconut palm sugar
¼ teaspoon ground cinnamon

Preheat the oven to 180°C/350°F/Gas mark 4. Line a 20cm x 20cm brownie tin with greaseproof paper.

TO MAKE THE CRUMBLE

To make the crumble, which will be used as the base and topping, whizz all the ingredients except the buckwheat flakes together in a food processor until the almonds are breaking down.

Add the buckwheat flakes and pulse until the mixture is still looking crumbly, but when you pinch it between your fingers it is tacky and holds its shape.

Put a little more than half of the mix in the brownie tin and spread until even, pressing down until really firm and solid.

TO MAKE THE APPLE FILLING

Cook all the ingredients for the apple filling together with 25ml water over a medium heat until the pieces of apple are soft, but still present.

Spread this over the crumble base, then sprinkle the remaining crumble mix over the top.

Bake in the oven for 10 minutes until the crumble topping starts to brown slightly.

Leave to cool completely before slicing into squares.

BANANA & PEANUT BUTTER CRUMBLE SQUARES

I love these crumble squares for treats on the weekends. They have the perfect level of sweetness and such a satisfying consistency.

Makes 12 Squares

CRUMBLE
200g jumbo oats
30g flaxseed
60g firm raw coconut oil
250g soft pitted Medjool dates
1/4 teaspoon salt
1/2 tablespoon cacao powder

BANANA FILLING
350g ripe peeled bananas
50g smooth peanut butter
1 1/2 tablespoons cacao powder

Preheat the oven to 180°C/350°F/Gas mark 4. Line a 20cm x 20cm brownie tin with greaseproof paper.

TO MAKE THE CRUMBLE
To make the crumble, which will be used as the base and topping, whizz all the ingredients together in a food processor until the mixture is still looking crumbly, but when you pinch it between your fingers it is tacky and holds its shape.

Put two-thirds of the mix into the brownie tin and spread until even, pressing it down until really firm and solid.

TO MAKE THE BANANA FILLING
Cook all the ingredients for the banana filling along with 100ml water on a hob over a medium heat for 10 minutes so that the bananas are breaking down and the mix is fairly thick.

Spread the banana mix over the crumble base, then sprinkle the remaining crumble mix over the top.

Bake in the oven for 10 minutes until the crumble topping starts to brown slightly.

Leave to cool completely before slicing into squares.

BERRY CRUMBLE SQUARES

{Nut Free}

Since the mixed berry and coconut crumble is probably my favourite flavour crumble out in stores, I wanted to include a similar recipe for this book. These crumble squares make an ideal breakfast bite or teatime snack.

Makes 12 Squares

CRUMBLE

120g jumbo oats, ground to
    an oatmeal before using
60g firm raw coconut oil
210g soft pitted Medjool dates
¼ teaspoon salt
¼ teaspoon vanilla powder
170g whole jumbo oats

BERRY FILLING

180g raspberries
180g blueberries
¼ teaspoon vanilla powder
30g white chia seeds

Preheat the oven to 180°C/350°F/Gas mark 4. Line a 20cm x 20cm brownie tin with greaseproof paper.

TO MAKE THE CRUMBLE

To make the crumble base and topping, whizz all the ingredients (except for the whole jumbo oats) together in a food processor until the mixture is still looking crumbly, but when you pinch it between your fingers it is tacky and holds its shape.

Add the whole jumbo oats to this mix and stir them in.

Put two-thirds of the mix in the brownie tin and spread out until even, pressing down until really firm and solid.

TO MAKE THE BERRY FILLING

Cook all the ingredients for the berry filling together with 1 tablespoon water over a medium heat for 15–20 minutes, until a thick compote is formed. The mixture should still have pieces of fruit in it.

Spread the berry mix over the crumble base, then sprinkle the remaining crumble mix over the top.

Bake in the oven for 10 minutes until the crumble topping starts to brown slightly.

Leave to cool completely before slicing into squares.

Biscuits and Cookies

CHOCOLATE CARAMEL BISCUIT FINGERS

{Nut Free}

Nothing quite beats a gooey caramel chocolate bar. Now my fridge is rarely without a stack of these and I love offering them to visitors and seeing their faces when they find out they are healthy. Everyone genuinely thinks they are better than a normal chocolate bar! What is also fun about this is that you can use whichever date caramel you like.

Makes about 10 Bars

BISCUITS

150g jumbo oats or oat flour

4 tablespoons melted raw
   coconut oil

75ml maple syrup

¼ teaspoon vanilla powder

½ Date Caramel recipe
   (page 61)

CHOCOLATE

65g cacao butter

40g cacao powder

½ teaspoon vanilla powder

pinch of salt

4 tablespoons maple syrup

Preheat the oven to 180°C/350°F/Gas mark 4.

TO MAKE THE BISCUITS

If using whole oats, blend to a fine flour-like powder.

Mix all the ingredients for the biscuits in the blender and then leave for 5–10 minutes to firm up.

Line a baking tray with greaseproof paper.

Shape the mixture into fingers and bake on the lined tray for 14–15 minutes until browning only very slightly on the top. They should still have a tiny bit of softness to them when they are taken out.

Leave to cool. The biscuits will firm further once cool.

Spread the Date Caramel onto the top of the biscuits.

TO MAKE THE CHOCOLATE

Melt the cacao butter in a bain-marie or a glass bowl sitting above, not touching, a pan of simmering water.

Add all the other ingredients, still over the heat, and stir for a minute or two until combined and glossy. Leave to cool slightly.

Dip the biscuits into the chocolate, place on the lined tray and refrigerate for about 1–2 hours until set. Store in the fridge if you want a crunchier biscuit.

Biscuits and Cookies

CHOCOLATE MALTED MACA BISCUITS

With Himalayan Pink Salt

{Nut Free}

I've managed to combine my love of maca with my love of chocolate biscuits and nothing could be better! These are perfect to make into little round biscuit balls or, if you prefer, you can make them into flatter, rounder biscuits. I designed these for my sister Hayley, who loves nothing more than a little chocolate biscuit after dinner.

Makes 10–12 Biscuits

BISCUITS

150g jumbo oats, ground to an oatmeal before using, or oat flour

35g melted raw coconut oil

75ml maple syrup

¼ teaspoon vanilla powder

2½ tablespoons maca powder

¾ Dark Chocolate recipe (page 54)

Himalayan pink salt, to sprinkle

Preheat the oven to 180°C/350°F/Gas mark 4.

TO MAKE THE BISCUITS

Add all the biscuit ingredients to a food processor and blend until the mixture comes together (you can also do this in a bowl with a spoon).

If the mixture is too soft to roll, leave for 5–10 minutes to firm up – don't worry if it is still slightly wet.

Line a baking tray with greaseproof paper.

Roll into balls, then flatten a little if you want a more cookie-like shape. Place onto the lined baking tray and bake for 9 minutes until the cookies begin to brown only slightly.

Leave the biscuits to cool.

Dip the cooled biscuits into the chocolate and sprinkle a little bit of Himalayan salt on the top.

Place in the fridge for 1–2 hours to set the chocolate.

Store in the fridge if you want a crunchier biscuit.

CHOCOLATE COCONUT BISCUIT BARS
{ *Nut Free* }

Chocolate and coconut are a match made in heaven! Desiccated coconut is added to the biscuit and to the chocolate, while coconut milk is also added to the chocolate to make it a little milkier and to guarantee that the taste of coconut is supreme.

Makes 8 Bars

BISCUITS

150g jumbo oats, ground to an oatmeal before using, or oat flour
35g melted raw coconut oil
75ml maple syrup
¼ teaspoon vanilla powder
30g finely desiccated coconut

CHOCOLATE

35g cacao butter
20g cacao powder
2 tablespoons maple syrup
¼ teaspoon vanilla powder
pinch of salt
45ml full-fat coconut milk – the hard creamy part from the top of a tin, not the water (don't use low-fat as these types will not have this cream)
25g finely desiccated coconut, plus extra to decorate

Preheat the oven to 180°C/350°F/Gas mark 4.

TO MAKE THE BISCUITS

Add all the ingredients except the desiccated coconut to a food processor. Blend until it comes together.

Stir or pulse in the desiccated coconut.

Line a baking tray with greaseproof paper.

Shape the mixture into fingers and bake on the lined tray for 14–15 minutes until browning only very slightly on the top. They should still have a tiny bit of softness to them when they are taken out.

Leave to cool. The biscuits will firm further once cool.

TO MAKE THE CHOCOLATE

Melt the cacao butter in a bain-marie or a glass bowl sitting above, not touching, a pan of simmering water.

Add all the other ingredients except the desiccated coconut and stir until smooth.

Add the desiccated coconut and dip the biscuits in.

Sprinkle a little more desiccated coconut on top and then refrigerate for 1–2 hours, leaving to set.

Store in the fridge if you want a crunchier biscuit.

Cookies

I seem to be saying this under each category, but cookies are something I absolutely could not live without! Dipping cookies into a big cup of tea is something I find very comforting. I'm such a big fan of cookies that I ended up calling our family dog Cookie, who is my absolute love.

CRUNCHY GINGER COOKIES
{Nut Free}

Everyone loves a simple tea-dunking cookie and these are perfect for this. My friend Kira and I always catch up over a cup of tea, and I really think that these cookies may have brought us closer! She seems a lot more available now she knows I always have these to offer. But I'm not complaining, that is what my food is all about – bringing people together! The ginger in these is really subtle and not overpowering at all.

Makes 8 Cookies

200g ground oats (grind jumbo oats to an oatmeal before using)
60g raw honey
2 teaspoons grated fresh ginger
1 teaspoon ground ginger
10g coconut palm sugar
sprinkle of ground nutmeg
pinch of salt
50g softened raw coconut oil

Preheat the oven to 180°C/350°F/Gas mark 4. Line a baking tray with greaseproof paper.

Mix all the ingredients together in a bowl.

Roll the mixture into balls and flatten into cookie shapes.

Place on the lined baking tray.

Bake for 20 minutes, turning them over after 10 minutes, until they are browning. The cookies become crunchier as they cool.

MACA & RAISIN COOKIES

{Nut Free}

The combination of maca and maple syrup gives the cookies an irresistible caramel-like flavour. The cookies themselves go a little crunchy, which is why the raisins complement them so well as they make the cookies chewy too. These are the cookies I brought with me to my publisher meetings, and here I am writing a book, so they must have done the trick!

Makes 8 Cookies

150g oat flour

150g jumbo oats

5 tablespoons melted coconut oil

150ml maple syrup

110g raisins

½ teaspoon salt

3 tablespoons maca powder

Preheat the oven to 180°C/350°F/Gas mark 4. Line a baking tray with greaseproof paper.

Mix all the ingredients together in a mixing bowl.

Make small cookie shapes out of the mix and place on the lined baking tray.

Bake for 8 minutes until they become a golden colour. The cookies should still be soft when taken out as they firm up quite a lot when cooled.

RAW CACAO & CAROB SANDWICH COOKIES

Now these are really special. The superfood powders in this recipe make the cookies not only rich and full of flavour, but wonderfully nourishing, too. What more could you want? These are pretty filling so are the perfect afternoon snack to keep you going.

Makes 14 Cookies

CASHEW CREAM FILLING
100g smooth cashew butter
½ tablespoon vanilla powder
1 tablespoon coconut palm sugar

COOKIES
110g flaxseed
150g ground almonds
100ml date syrup
25g melted raw coconut oil
¼ teaspoon salt
2 tablespoons carob powder
2 tablespoons cacao powder
½ tablespoon vanilla powder
1 tablespoon coconut sugar

TO MAKE THE CASHEW CREAM FILLING
Mix all the ingredients together in a bowl.

TO MAKE THE COOKIES
Put all the ingredients in a mixing bowl. Using your hands, mix together well until all combined and sticky.

Using your hands, roll out the mixture into small cookie shapes. To do this, make a big marble-size ball of mix and then roll and press into a cookie shape. You need to put a lot of pressure on them with your palms to make them nice and flat.

Once all the mixture has been used and all the cookies have been shaped, using a knife, spread the cashew cream on a cookie and place another cookie on top. Repeat until you have used up all the mixture and filling.

OAT & RAISIN COOKIES

The most comforting cookie of all time! Perfectly crisp on the outside and chewy in the middle. These are wonderful for dipping in tea and to enjoy on a colder, rainy day.

Makes 10 Large Cookies

185g almond butter

150g apple purée or unsweetened apple sauce

100g jumbo oats

100g rolled oats

150ml maple syrup

150g raisins

1½ teaspoons ground cinnamon

pinch of salt

Preheat the oven to 180°C/350°F/Gas mark 4.

Mix all the ingredients together in a bowl. It will be quite a wet consistency at this stage.

Roll the mixture into balls and then squash so that they are biscuit-shaped.

Place on a lined baking tray and bake in the oven for 20–22 minutes.

PEANUT BUTTER & CHOCOLATE COOKIES

The texture of these cookies is perfection, as is the flavour combination of smooth peanut butter and cacao. They are not too rich and are totally addictive.

Makes about 10 cookies

15 soft pitted Medjool dates
25ml boiling water
4 tablespoons cacao powder
75g oat flour
25g finely desiccated coconut
25ml maple syrup
10g cacao nibs
150g smooth runny peanut butter
pinch of salt

Preheat the oven to 180°C/350°F/Gas mark 4. Line a baking tray with greaseproof paper.

Mix the dates with the boiling water and the cacao powder until a thick paste is formed.

Put this in a mixing bowl, add in the other ingredients and stir well until combined.

Roll the mixture into balls and flatten to biscuit shapes. Arrange on the lined tray.

Bake for 10 minutes. When the cookies come out of the oven, they should be soft. They firm slightly as they cool, but the middle should remain soft.

RAW GINGER COOKIES

{ *Nut Free* }

I used to think the best cookies were those that were fresh out of the oven and still hot. I didn't realise how tasty raw cookies can be, not to mention so super easy to make! Here I have put a slight twist on ginger snaps, making them less 'snap' like and more sticky. I love using fresh ginger in sweet recipes like this one, not only for the taste, but for the amazing health benefits it provides. A real wonder spice, ginger is thought to be very effective in reducing nausea, morning sickness, pain and inflammation.

Makes about 12 Cookies

2 tablespoons flaxseed
150g jumbo oats
30g buckwheat groats
50ml maple syrup
200g soft pitted Medjool dates
1¼ teaspoons grated fresh ginger
15g white chia seeds
pinch of ground nutmeg

Mix the flaxseed with 4–6 tablespoons water and leave to set for 10 minutes until a thick jelly-like consistency is formed. This is known as a flax egg and helps to bind ingredients.

Mix all the ingredients together in a food processor.

Roll into thick, round cookies.

Pies and Tarts

PECAN PIE

Pecan pie will always remind me of one of my best friends, Rose. I went travelling with Rose when I was 18 all around Australia and New Zealand and whenever we would stop for anything sweet, she would always opt for a slice of pecan pie. During this time pecan pie was not my first choice, but when Rose made a permanent move to Australia last year, she asked me to make a pecan pie recipe and send it over to her. Since then, I have a new-found love for it. What is really special about this recipe is that it can be totally raw if you prefer, or the base can be baked to be a little crispier.

Makes a 24cm Pie

softened coconut oil, for greasing the tin
Sticky Nut Crust, raw or cooked (page 49)

TOPPING
Pecan and Maca Butter (page 47)
10–15 whole pecans, to decorate

Grease a deep 24cm pie dish and, using your hands, spread the crust out evenly across it.

TO MAKE THE TOPPING
Spoon out the Pecan and Maca Butter filling into the Sticky Nut Crust and smooth over evenly with your palms.

Decorate with the whole pecan nuts.

APPLE PIE

{ *Nut Free* }

There were very high standards to meet in my house when it came to apple pie. My Grandma used to make my Dad an apple pie every year for his birthday, and it was his favourite treat. When I dug out her recipe to find out how she made it, I wasn't surprised to find that she used pounds and pounds of butter and sugar. It was definitely a challenge to come up with a recipe that my Dad would say was better, but, very happily, I have achieved it here. The combination of the baked apple slices in maca-infused date toffee, sitting on top of the Ultimate Pastry, took his breath away.

Makes a 24cm Pie

softened coconut oil, for greasing the tin
2 x Ultimate Pastry recipe (page 48)

FILLING

300g soft pitted Medjool dates
2 tablespoons maca powder
1 tablespoon ground cinnamon
75g apple purée or unsweetened apple sauce
1 teaspoon ground ginger
50g raw coconut oil

TOPPING

3–4 Granny Smith apples
½ tablespoon coconut palm sugar
pinch of ground cinnamon

Continued ››

Preheat the oven to 180°C/350°F/Gas mark 4.

Grease a 24cm pie tin with the coconut oil. Weigh out 400g of the pastry dough and roll into a ball.

Roll out with a rolling pin until a small circle shape is formed.

Place in the greased pie tin and, using your hands, flatten the pastry out across the tin and along the sides, making sure it is spread evenly.

TO MAKE THE FILLING

Put the soft dates in a food processor and add all the other filling ingredients. Blend until the mixture is well combined, sticky and thick.

Spread evenly across the pastry base using a spoon.

TO MAKE THE TOPPING

Core and slice the apples and arrange evenly over the entire pie, sinking the apples into the sticky filling.

Roll the remaining dough mix into a ball with your hands, ensuring your hands are cool as hot hands will make the pastry crumble.

Sprinkle some oat flour on the surface before you roll it out.

Using a rolling pin, roll out the dough until really thin and in a circle shape.

Cut out long strips and place over the pie, weaving the strips across each other.

Sprinkle over the coconut palm sugar and a pinch of ground cinnamon.

Place in the oven and bake for 40–45 minutes.

PUMPKIN PIE

A few years ago I spent Thanksgiving in LA and it was enough to make me
a pumpkin pie convert for life. A slice of this with a cup of tea is so heavenly
in the Autumn!

Makes a 24cm Pie

softened coconut oil, for
   greasing the dish
Ultimate Pastry or Sticky Nut
   Crust (pages 48 and 49), with
   1 teaspoon ground cinnamon
   added

PUMPKIN FILLING

200g soft pitted Medjool dates
425g tin pumpkin purée
1 teaspoon ground cinnamon
¼ teaspoon ground nutmeg
¼ teaspoon ground ginger
¼ teaspoon salt
½ Blanched Almond Vanilla
   Butter recipe (page 46)
50ml maple syrup, plus extra
   for glazing
1 tablespoon flaked almonds,
   to decorate

Preheat the oven to 180°C/350°F/Gas mark 4.

Grease a deep 24cm pie dish and, using your
hands, spread the pastry or crust out evenly across
it.

TO MAKE THE PUMPKIN FILLING

Add to a food processor all of the ingredients
for the pumpkin filling and mix until well
incorporated. This can also be done in a bowl.

Spread the pumpkin mixture over the pastry and
bake in the oven for 30 minutes until the filling
has begun to brown slightly around the outside.
The filling should still feel bouncy and soft, but
not wet.

Brush a maple syrup glaze over the whole pie and
sprinkle the flaked almonds over the top to serve.

APRICOT TART

Apricots by themselves are not a fruit I regularly eat, but when experimenting with fruits for this chapter, apricots were amongst the clear winners. I love the beauty of this tart just as much as the taste.

Makes a 24cm Tart

softened coconut oil, for greasing the dish
Ultimate Pastry or Sticky Nut Crust (pages 48 and 49)
300g fresh apricots (250g when stoned), thinly sliced

FILLING
350g fresh apricots (300g when stoned)
200g Blanched Almond Vanilla Butter (page 46)
65ml maple syrup
1 teaspoon vanilla powder

GLAZE
2 tablespoons maple syrup
1 tablespoon raw coconut oil
¼ teaspoon vanilla powder

Preheat the oven to 180°C/350°F/Gas mark 4.

Grease a 24cm tart tin and, using your hands, spread the pastry or crust out evenly across it. Bake in the oven for 8 minutes until it begins to firm and brown slightly.

TO MAKE THE FILLING
Blend the 300g stoned apricots to a purée, then add the other filling ingredients and blend until smooth.

Spread this filling into the pie case.

Arrange the stoned and thinly sliced apricots on top of the filling.

TO MAKE THE GLAZE
Mix up all the ingredients for the glaze and brush it over the apricots.

Bake for 25 minutes until the filling and apricots are golden.

CHRISTMAS MINCE PIES

{Nut Free}

It is rare to have any sort of room for dessert after the mammoth Christmas meal that most of us enjoy, but trust me, you should leave a little room for these.

Makes 6–8 Mince Pies

softened coconut oil, for greasing the tins
3 x Ultimate Pastry recipe (page 48), with 2 teaspoons ground cinnamon, ½ teaspoon ground cloves, ½ teaspoon ground nutmeg and ½ teaspoon grated fresh ginger or ground ginger added
1½ tablespoons maple syrup, to brush
coconut palm sugar, to sprinkle

MINCEMEAT FILLING
4 red apples, peeled, cored and chopped
zest of 1 large orange
125g raisins
30g coconut palm sugar
¼ teaspoon ground cloves
¼ teaspoon ground nutmeg
1 teaspoon ground cinnamon

Preheat the oven to 180°C/350°F/Gas mark 4.

Grease one or two muffin tins with coconut oil.

Line the tins with two-thirds of the pastry, leaving the tops open.

Roll out the remaining pastry and use a round cutter to cut out lids and a star-shaped cutter to cut out decorations. Set aside for now.

TO MAKE THE MINCEMEAT FILLING
Boil all the mincemeat ingredients in a saucepan with 100ml water for 15–20 minutes over a medium-high heat, stirring occasionally.

Fill the pastry cases with the mincemeat and cover with the pastry tops, pressing the edges down. Place a pastry star on the top of each lid.

Brush the pastry tops with maple syrup and sprinkle coconut palm sugar on top.

Bake for 30 minutes until the tops begin to look golden and crunchy.

When cool, sprinkle over a little extra coconut sugar and serve.

MOCHA MOUSSE TART

This dessert has quite a sophisticated flavour and is perfect to serve at dinner parties. The avocado makes the mousse creamy, however the taste is masked by the cacao and coffee, which work so well together! I dedicate this recipe to two of my very special friends, Patti and Ari, who love tarts and pies, and this one in particular!

Makes a 24cm Tart

softened coconut oil, for greasing the tin
Sticky Nut Crust (page 49)

TOPPING
3 tablespoons cacao butter
5 tablespoons instant coffee
200ml maple syrup
4 tablespoons cacao powder
2½ ripe avocados
30g buckwheat flour

Grease a deep 24cm tart tin and, using your hands, spread the crust out evenly across it.

TO MAKE THE TOPPING
In a pan, melt the cacao butter over a low heat.

In another pan, heat the coffee, maple syrup and cacao powder together.

Add the avocado flesh, liquid coffee mix, cacao butter and buckwheat flour to a food processor and blend together until smooth and creamy.

Spoon the filling into the Sticky Nut Crust base and refrigerate to set.

Keep refrigerated until ready to serve.

BERRY TARTLETS

Not only do these taste so amazing, but they look beyond beautiful and are perfect for serving at a tea party. Of course, this recipe could be made into a single large tart if you prefer.

Makes 5 Tartlets

softened coconut oil, for greasing the tin
Ultimate Pastry (page 48)
200g mixed berries (75g raspberries, 25g blueberries and 100g strawberries)

VANILLA COCONUT CREAM

200ml thick Oat Milk (page 44)
400ml tin full-fat coconut milk – the hard creamy part from the top of a tin, not the water (don't use low-fat as these types will not have this cream)
½ teaspoon vanilla powder
3 tablespoons coconut palm sugar

Preheat the oven to 180°C/350°F/Gas mark 4.

Grease five 10cm tartlet tins and divide the pastry equally between the tins.

Bake the pastry cases for 10 minutes until firm.

TO MAKE THE VANILLA COCONUT CREAM

Cook all the vanilla coconut cream ingredients together in a pan, stirring constantly, over a high heat for 5 minutes, or until thick.

Pour the mixture onto the baked pastry cases and then assemble the berries on top.

CHOCOLATE & ORANGE CARAMEL CAKE TART

This cake tart was inspired by the well-known 'Jaffa Cake'. I took this concept and made it my own. Here the orange layer is sandwiched between a nutty tart base and a thin chocolate torte layer. If you are a chocolate orange fan like me, this is definitely the cake you should make!

Makes a 24cm Tart

softened coconut oil,
    for greasing the tin
Sticky Nut Crust (page 49)
Orange Caramel (page 61)
zest of 1 orange, to sprinkle

CHOCOLATE TORTE
125g soft pitted Medjool dates
3 tablespoons cacao powder
125g almond butter
150g Oat Milk (or Almond Milk)
    (page 44 and 42)

Preheat the oven to 180°C/350°F/Gas mark 4.

Grease a 24cm tart tin. Line with the crust and bake in the oven for 8 minutes until it begins to firm and brown slightly.

Spoon the Orange Caramel over the Sticky Nut Crust.

TO MAKE THE CHOCOLATE TORTE
Mix all the ingredients for the chocolate torte in a food processor and then place over the Orange Caramel.

Bake the cake tart in the oven for 15–20 minutes until the chocolate torte is firm but not too hard.

Leave to set in the fridge for at least 30 minutes before serving.

Sprinkle the orange zest over the top.

Puddings

BAKED PEANUT BUTTER CHOCOLATE POTS

No matter how generous or filling a main meal may be, for me there is always room for dessert, and sometimes all I want is for that dessert to be deeply chocolatey. This is the recipe to use when it is that kind of night.

Makes 6 Pots

softened coconut oil, for greasing the dishes
250g soft pitted Medjool dates
8 tablespoons cacao powder
350g peanut butter
1 avocado
300ml Oat Milk (page 44)
¼ teaspoon salt
3 tablespoons coconut palm sugar, plus extra for dusting

Preheat the oven to 180°C/350°F/Gas mark 4. Grease six pots or soufflé dishes with coconut oil.

Blend all the ingredients in a food processor until well mixed.

Pour the mixture evenly into the pots, dust with some extra coconut sugar and place in the oven.

Bake for 12–14 minutes. Best served hot.

APPLE & GOOSEBERRY CRUMBLE

Apple crumble is the most traditional crumble of all. The conventional recipe is made with a lot of caster sugar, butter and flour. This recipe uses different ingredients, yet achieves the same wonderful textures. The gooseberry makes the apple compote a little tart, but it is perfectly balanced with the addition of the sweet millet and pecan maple topping. I adore this recipe served warm on winter evenings.

Serves 8

FRUIT COMPOTE

550g Bramley apples
500g gooseberries
4 tablespoons coconut
    palm sugar
1 tablespoon ground
    cinnamon

CRUMBLE TOPPING

220g pecans
½ tablespoon ground
    cinnamon
pinch of salt
120g millet flakes
40g raw coconut oil
70ml maple syrup

Preheat the oven to 180°C/350°F/Gas mark 4.

TO MAKE THE FRUIT COMPOTE

Peel and dice the apples.

Heat in a saucepan over a medium-high heat.

Add all the other fruit compote ingredients and stir well.

Leave on the heat for about 20–25 minutes until the fruit has broken down into a purée and only some chunks still remain.

TO MAKE THE CRUMBLE TOPPING

Make the crumble by blending 120g of the pecans with the cinnamon and salt in a food processor until a flour is formed. Put this in a bowl and add the millet flakes.

Add the remaining 100g pecans to the food processor and pulse until the pecans have broken down, but are still in chunks. Add this to the bowl with the ground pecans and millet flakes.

Melt the coconut oil and add this to the bowl along with the maple syrup and stir well.

Pour the fruit mixture into an ovenproof dish and then cover the top with crumble.

Bake for 20 minutes to crisp up.

APPLE MOUSSE

{ Nut Free }

This recipe will forever remind me of my parents. My Grandma (on my Dad's side) used to love anything appley. She would regularly serve apple mousse after a meal, so it has always been one of his favourite desserts. Coincidentally, it was something my Mum grew up with too. She started making apple mousse for us as babies, and as we were growing up it was one of mine and my sisters' top desserts. It is perfectly sweet and light.

Serves 4

3 large Bramley apples
40g coconut palm sugar
10 whole cloves

Peel the apples, core and cut into small chunks.

Place the apple, sugar, cloves and 1 tablespoon water in a saucepan and gently heat until boiling. Turn the heat down and simmer for about 20 minutes until the apples fall apart.

Carefully remove the cloves, ensuring all are out.

Using a hand-held blender, blitz the mixture into a purée.

Allow to cool.

Serve the mousse in individual bowls or glasses.

ORANGES IN CARAMEL

{ *Nut Free* }

This is a perfect palate cleanser after a big meal, when you still fancy something sweet. It is a sophisticated dish yet it couldn't be more simple.

Serves 4

100g coconut palm sugar

4 large oranges

Warm a saucepan over a medium heat for 5 minutes. Once warmed, place the sugar in the saucepan.

Continuing with a medium heat, leave the sugar to warm for 5 minutes, then shake the pan to move it around.

Leave for another 5 minutes and start to stir the sugar gently and continuously for 10 minutes until the granules have become liquid. You should see a creamy consistency and a medium-brown colour. Stir very gently so that none of the sugar moves away from the heat. If it does, it will become rock hard and stick to the sides of the pan.

Once the granules have melted into the creamy mixture, put on oven gloves to protect your hands as you very gently pour in 4 tablespoons warm water, stirring all the time. It will bubble and spatter a little, but once the water is stirred in, it will become dark and clear. Allow to cool.

On a chopping board, cut off the bottom and top of the oranges and then cut all the rind and pith away from the rest of the oranges. Lay the peeled oranges on their sides and slice each one into about five slices. Reshape the oranges and secure with a wooden cocktail stick.

Place the oranges either in individual bowls or one very large bowl, and gently pour over the caramel sauce, leaving a little of the bright orange showing.

If caramel has stuck to the pan, fill the pan with water and pour in a good amount of salt. Bring almost to a boil and stir all the time until the sugar melts and the pan is clean.

RAW CHOCOLATE & MACA MOLTEN LAVA CAKES

In previous years, if a restaurant served chocolate fondant as a dessert, I would always choose it. The sensation of breaking into a domed pudding with a spoon and seeing chocolate sauce oozing out never got old. Somehow, I had to recreate this experience so that I could still enjoy the pleasures of a fondant. This molten lava cake is raw, requiring no baking at all (although it can be slightly heated in a low oven for 10 minutes if preferred).

Makes 6 Cakes

softened coconut oil, for greasing
   the dishes

CAKES
200g blanched almonds
70g rolled oats
325g soft pitted Medjool dates
4½ tablespoons cacao powder
4 tablespoons maca powder
3 tablespoons maple syrup
¼ teaspoon salt

MOLTEN SAUCE
1 ripe avocado
6 tablespoons maple syrup
3 tablespoons cacao powder
3 tablespoons maca powder
4 tablespoons almond butter
2 tablespoons softened raw
   coconut oil

Grease the muffin tins with coconut oil.

TO MAKE THE CAKES

Mix all the cake ingredients in a food processor until well mixed and sticky.

Using your hands, use three-quarters of the mix to line each hole in a muffin tin with the mixture, covering the bottom and the sides of the hole only and leaving the top open. Alternatively, use rubber muffin moulds if you have them.

TO MAKE THE MOLTEN SAUCE

Make the sauce by mixing all the ingredients in a food processor until thick, creamy and well mixed.

Spoon 2 tablespoons of the sauce into each cake case and then cover with the remaining cake mix as a lid, ensuring the edges are stuck together.

Turn out the cakes to serve.

RAW TIRAMISU

Tiramisu was always in demand in my family, but I was never a fan of the mascarpone, so I tended to shy away from it. I loved the sound of everything else about it though, and so have taken inspiration from the conventional recipe and put a little spin on it to create something a bit different. This version of tiramisu is now up there on my favourites list.

Serves 10–12

LADYFINGER LAYER
250g pecans
250g rolled oats
10 teaspoons instant coffee
¼ teaspoon vanilla powder
250g soft pitted Medjool dates
50g raisins
pinch of salt
2 tablespoons carob powder (optional)

CHOCOLATE MOUSSE LAYER
250g cashews
150g soft pitted Medjool dates
4 tablespoons maple syrup
40g melted raw coconut oil
2 x 400ml tins full-fat coconut milk – the hard creamy part from the top of a tin, not the water (don't use low-fat as these types will not have this cream)
6 tablespoons cacao powder
pinch of salt
2 tablespoons instant coffee

VANILLA CREAM LAYER
340g cashews
1 tablespoon vanilla powder
40g melted raw coconut oil
4 tablespoons maple syrup
100ml coconut water from the open coconut milk tins

instant coffee powder, cacao powder and coconut palm sugar, to decorate

Continued »

Soak all the cashews overnight or for a minimum of 4–6 hours. Drain and rinse.

TO MAKE THE LADYFINGER LAYER

Mix all the ladyfinger ingredients in a food processor.

Place two-thirds of the mixture in a deep dish, pressing down so that you have a flat layer, and leave to set in the freezer for at least 2 hours.

TO MAKE THE CHOCOLATE MOUSSE LAYER

Make the chocolate mousse layer by mixing all the ingredients together in a food processor until smooth and thick. Spread this mixture evenly across the frozen ladyfinger base.

Set in the freezer for another 30 minutes.

TO MAKE THE VANILLA CREAM LAYER

Make the vanilla cream by blending all the ingredients together in the food processor until smooth and thick.

With the remaining third of the ladyfinger mixture, make ladyfinger shapes using your hands and place on top of the chocolate mousse layer.

Pour the vanilla cream over the layer of ladyfinger shapes.

Sprinkle a pinch of instant coffee and cacao powders and coconut palm sugar over the vanilla cream to decorate and then set in the freezer for at least 5–6 hours.

Take the tiramisu out of the freezer and refrigerate for at least 2 hours before serving to allow the dessert to defrost slightly.

CARDAMOM, COCONUT & BROWN RICE PUDDING

{Nut Free}

Rice pudding made with white rice, cream and sugar is another traditional British dessert, but it is also a dish found in lots of other countries where it is made in different ways. In Asia, they often use brown or black rice to make their rice pudding. I decided to take inspiration from them and use brown rice instead of white due to its higher nutritional content. Brown rice is a grain that still has its husk and bran, which are rich in calcium, magnesium and fibre, while the cardamom in this recipe adds further nutritional value. This dish is delicious served hot or cold.

Serves 8

440g short-grain brown rice, washed
400ml tin coconut milk
2–3 cardamom pods
100ml maple syrup
¾ teaspoon ground cinnamon, plus extra for dusting
¼ teaspoon ground nutmeg, plus extra for dusting

Cook the rice in the coconut milk, mixed with 400ml water, as per the cooking instructions.

Whilst the rice is cooking, grind the cardamom pods in a pestle and mortar, removing and discarding the husks.

Once the rice is cooked, add all the remaining ingredients into the saucepan of rice and mix well.

Stir continuously over a medium heat for 20 minutes until the mixture becomes creamy.

Serve dusted with a little ground cinnamon and nutmeg.

SUMMER PEACH CRUMBLE

{Nut Free}

In the summer of 2015, I introduced a limited edition peach crumble to the stores. It did so well, and customers were so sad to learn it was only available for a short period of time, that I've decided to share a slightly altered recipe here. This crumble topping is nut free, which makes it slightly lighter. Since the topping is predominantly made from oats, this crumble has become one of my favourite breakfasts of all time.

Serves 8

FILLING

800g stoned and chopped
   peaches (skins on)
100ml maple syrup
1 teaspoon vanilla powder

CRUMBLE TOPPING

200g ground oats (grind jumbo
   oats to an oatmeal before
   using) or oat flour
200g jumbo oats
5 tablespoons melted raw
   coconut oil
100ml maple syrup
$^1/_8$ teaspoon salt
$1^1/_2$ teaspoons vanilla powder

coconut yoghurt, to serve

Preheat the oven to 180°C/350°F/Gas mark 4.

TO MAKE THE FILLING

Cook the peaches in a saucepan over a medium to low heat with the maple syrup and vanilla powder. Cook for about 20 minutes or until soft.

TO MAKE THE CRUMBLE TOPPING

To a mixing bowl, add the ground oats or oat flour, jumbo oats, coconut oil, maple syrup, salt and vanilla powder and mix thoroughly.

Once the filling is nice and soft, add to an ovenproof dish and top with the crumble mixture.

Bake for 20 minutes until the topping begins to brown.

Serve with a dollop of coconut yoghurt.

CHOPPED FRESH FRUIT SALAD

{Nut Free}

I have to give my Mum all the credit for this recipe. This is something she has served at every Friday night dinner with my family for as long as I can remember. She never added any sugars or juices and always spent so much time preparing the chopped fruit beautifully. This fruit salad is simply the best I have ever had. The different fruits complement each other so well, with my favourite definitely being the pomegranate seeds for a little crunch!

Serves 8

FRUIT

150g mango
200g pineapple
200g melon (orange and green)
2 kiwis
150g red or green grapes
80g blackberries

SAUCE

juice from 1 large orange
60g pomegranate seeds
2 passion fruits

Cut the fruit into small chunks and place in a bowl of your choice.

To make the sauce, add the orange juice to the pomegranate seeds and flesh from the passion fruits.

Add this to the fruit salad bowl.

You can also add watermelon, strawberries and peaches, if you desire.

POACHED PEARS

{Nut Free}

Simple yet sophisticated, poached pears are such a lovely, light dessert to serve after an evening meal.

Serves 4

100ml cider vinegar
120g coconut palm sugar
4 large ripe pears, peeled but with stalks left in place
7 whole cloves
1 whole cinnamon stick

Put the cider vinegar, 300ml water and the coconut palm sugar in a saucepan and mix until the sugar is dissolved. Bring to the boil and then turn down to a simmer. At this stage the vinegar will burn off and will smell quite strong. This will fade after a short while. Simmer for 5 minutes.

Place the pears in the saucepan with the liquid and add the cloves and the cinnamon stick. Cover the pan with a lid and simmer for 10 minutes, then test with a small cocktail stick to see if the pears are tender. Cook for longer if necessary – the stick should easily enter the pears when they are cooked.

Carefully remove the pears with a large serving spoon and place in a serving dish.

Remove the cloves, counting to ensure all seven have been removed, and the cinnamon stick.

Pour the liquid over the pears and allow to cool before storing in the fridge.

The poached pears keep for 1–2 days and the flavour is improved one day after cooking.

CHOCOLATE ORANGE CRUMBLE

Since chocolate-orange is such a popular combination, I had to somehow make these flavours work in my signature dessert. This crumble is not the most conventional, but it is as delicious, if not more so, as the more traditional flavours you may have already tried. You have to give this one a go!

Serves 8

FRUIT COMPOTE

350g apple purée or
    unsweetened apple sauce
200g chopped oranges
4 tablespoons coconut
    palm sugar

CRUMBLE TOPPING

100g ground almonds
50g ground pecans
175g jumbo oats
50g melted raw coconut oil
100ml maple syrup
4 tablespoons cacao powder
zest of ½ orange
pinch of salt

Preheat the oven to 180°C/350°F/Gas mark 4.

TO MAKE THE FRUIT COMPOTE
Add all the fruit compote ingredients to a saucepan and cook over a medium heat for 10–20 minutes until they are softened.

TO MAKE THE CRUMBLE TOPPING
To make the crumble, combine all the ingredients in a bowl until well mixed.

Spoon the fruit compote into an ovenproof dish and then top with the crumble.

Bake for 15–20 minutes until the crumble topping begins to brown.

LEMON MOUSSE

This recipe is truly unique, and is one of the lighter options in this chapter. The lemon comes through so strongly in this mousse and is incredibly refreshing. It is a perfect dessert to serve after a really flavoursome meal as it helps to clear the palate.

Serves 8

4 ripe avocados
juice of 5 lemons
zest of 3 lemons
5 tablespoons maple syrup
3 tablespoons almond butter
berries and/or lemon zest, to serve

Mix all the ingredients in a food processor for 2 minutes until mixed well and creamy.

Serve the mousse with berries and/or a sprinkling of lemon zest.

STICKY NUT & DATE PUDDINGS

This is inspired by sticky toffee pudding, one of the most comforting and enticing desserts out there. After many, many attempts at trying to achieve a perfect pudding consistency for this recipe, I finally conquered it, and since then this has been a dessert in constant demand from friends and family.

Makes 5 Puddings

small amount of softened coconut oil, for greasing the tin

PUDDINGS

40g melted raw coconut oil
80g coconut palm sugar
150ml Almond Milk (page 42)
200g soft pitted Medjool dates
115g oat flour, ground oats
    (grind jumbo oats to an
    oatmeal before using) or
    ground almonds
115g pecans
½ teaspoon ground cinnamon

TOFFEE SAUCE

80ml date syrup
40g raw coconut oil
40g coconut palm sugar
50ml Almond Milk (page 42)
4 tablespoons almond butter
    (store-bought works best here
    as it is slightly runnier)

Preheat the oven to 180°C/350°F/Gas mark 4.

Grease a muffin tin with coconut oil.

TO MAKE THE PUDDINGS

Blend all the ingredients for the puddings in a food processor until they come together and the mixture is fairly smooth.

Spoon into the muffin tins.

Bake for 25 minutes until the puddings turn golden and firm with a good bounce.

TO MAKE THE TOFFEE SAUCE

Whilst the puddings are baking, add all the sauce ingredients to a pan and cook over a medium heat until the sauce is bubbling and has come together.

When the puddings are ready to serve, spoon about 2 tablespoons of the sauce over each one. Best served hot.

BAKED APPLES WITH PECANS & A MAPLE DRIZZLE

I adore this recipe with one of my cashew ice creams. The hot, sweet apples mixed with the cold ice cream forms a dreamy combination and a perfect dessert option.

Serves 4

4 good-size eating apples

STUFFING

40g pecans, coarsely chopped
20g rolled oats
30g coconut palm sugar
good pinch of ground cinnamon

BASTING LIQUID

30ml maple syrup

Preheat the oven to 180°C/350°F/Gas mark 4.

Using a long, thin knife or an apple corer, remove the cores from the apples.

FOR THE STUFFING

Grind the pecans and oats in a blender until they are in small pieces, then mix them together with the coconut palm sugar and the cinnamon.

Stuff the cavity in the apples with the mixture and place into an ovenproof, tight-fitting dish. If there is leftover stuffing, put the mixture on the bottom of the dish and sit the apples on top.

FOR THE BASTING LIQUID

For the basting liquid, mix 30ml water with the maple syrup and pour over the apples.

Bake for 40–45 minutes, basting the apples every 10 minutes.

The dish is ready when the apples are soft. Serve the apples with the basting liquid drizzled over.

Sweet Bites

MACA QUINOA CRISPIES

These are some of the bite-size treats that everyone, especially kids, love. Puffed quinoa has a similar consistency to puffed rice, which is used in classic chocolate rice crispies. Instead of using chocolate, I use maca in this recipe, alongside maple syrup, which gives the crispies a caramel-like flavour. These are the perfect snack to serve at tea and kids' parties.

Makes 8 Crispies

3 tablespoons maca powder
4 tablespoons raw coconut oil
6 tablespoons maple syrup
3 heaped tablespoons almond butter
¼ teaspoon salt
60g quinoa pops

Put all the ingredients except the quinoa pops in a saucepan and cook over a gentle heat until the mixture is hot and has become a runny liquid. Take off the heat before it starts bubbling.

Pour the mixture over the puffed quinoa and stir together until the mixture covers all of the quinoa.

Make ball shapes out of the quinoa mix, place in little fairy cake cases and arrange on a baking tray.

Leave to set in the fridge for 30 minutes.

MATCHA &
CACAO TRUFFLES

These make the most wonderful afternoon pick-me-up. When I
feel that my energy levels are really slumping, these little balls of
goodness are something I love to have to keep me going.

Makes 10–12 Truffles

210g blanched almonds
200g soft pitted Medjool dates
1 tablespoon matcha powder
5 tablespoons cacao powder
25g cacao nibs
pinch of salt

Mix all the ingredients in a food processor until the nuts are finely
chopped and the mixture is sticky.

Roll the mixture into balls.

You can keep these truffles in the fridge or in an airtight container
at room temperature.

CACAO &
MACA POPCORN

{ Nut Free }

Snacking on popcorn whilst working has always been a little habit
of mine. I did it when pulling all-nighters studying at university and
I still do it now when sitting at my laptop working on the business.
Popcorn, maca and chocolate are three ingredients I don't think I
could live without.

Serves 6

75g melted raw coconut oil
100g popcorn kernels
3 tablespoons coconut palm sugar
¼ teaspoon salt
1 tablespoon cacao powder
1 tablespoon maca powder

Heat 10g of the 75g coconut oil in a pan over a medium heat, then add
the kernels.

Cover the pan immediately with a lid and let the kernels pop, shaking
constantly so that they don't burn.

When all the kernels have popped, transfer the popcorn to a bowl.

Pour the remaining coconut oil, coconut palm sugar, salt, cacao
powder and maca on top and stir in.

PECAN, ORANGE & CHIA TRUFFLES

The orange and dates together in this recipe bring the ideal level of sweetness and highlight the flavour of the pecans so well. The chia seed coating on these gives some extra nutritional goodness and also a crunchy coating that makes them that much more satisfying and fun to eat!

Makes 15–18 Truffles

200g pecans
100ml fresh orange juice
200g soft pitted Medjool dates
zest of 1 orange
pinch of salt
50g white chia seeds

Mix together all of the ingredients except for the chia seeds in a food processor. Please note this mixture is quite moist.

Roll the mixture into balls.

Pour the chia seeds into a bowl and then roll the balls in the chia seeds so they are covered.

Place in the freezer to firm up a bit.

These truffles are best served straight from the freezer.

SALTED TAHINI &
COCONUT FUDGE

{ Nut Free }

I am completely in love with this recipe. Tahini (made from ground
sesame seeds) is a versatile and delicious ingredient to use in baking.
Through lots of experimentation, I've found that salting it and mixing
it with coconut brings out its flavour in a subtle way, reducing its
natural richness and providing it with an extra little bite.

Makes 14 Fudge Squares

60g tahini
150g soft pitted Medjool dates
2 tablespoons maple syrup
80g finely desiccated coconut
1½ tablespoons raw coconut oil
pinch of salt

Mix all the ingredients in a food processor until they
come together.

Place the mixture into a lined 11cm x 20cm loaf tin, flattening down
the top with your hands or the back of a spoon.

Place in the freezer for 30 minutes. Cut the fudge into squares or
rectangles and store in the fridge.

PISTACHIO & MATCHA BALLS

I love to have a couple of these a few hours before I work out. They are really satisfying, have just the right level of sweetness, and keep my energy levels high for an intense workout.

Makes 18–20 Smallish Balls

180g unsalted pistachio kernels

2 tablespoons matcha powder

100g finely desiccated coconut

200g soft pitted Medjool dates

2 tablespoons raw coconut oil

¼ teaspoon vanilla powder

juice of ½ lime

pinch of salt

Add all of the ingredients to a food processor and blend until the mixture comes together when squeezed.

Roll into balls and then place in the fridge to firm up.

PEANUT BUTTER BROWN RICE CRISPIES

These are similar to the traditional rice crispies but are made with puffed brown rice as opposed to puffed white rice since it hosts more nutritional value. When these puffs are coated with a sweet peanut butter sauce and put in the fridge to cool you are left with little bites of heaven!

Makes about 12–15 Crispies

150g peanut butter
100ml maple syrup
25g raw coconut oil
75g puffed brown rice

Heat the peanut butter, maple syrup and coconut oil in a pan until well mixed and liquid-like.

Pour the mixture over the puffed rice and stir until all the rice is well covered.

Spoon the mixture into fairy cake cases and leave to set in the fridge for about 30 minutes.

CHRISTMAS POPCORN

{Nut Free}

I love a family Christmas and I am never happier than when snuggled up on the sofa with my sisters and a duvet, watching a Christmas movie. I wanted to be able to add a little something to this essential Christmas pastime, and so I created a unique festive popcorn to be snacked on in front of the TV.

Serves 6

75g melted raw coconut oil
100g popcorn kernels
3 tablespoons coconut palm sugar
½ teaspoon ground cinnamon
¼ teaspoon ground nutmeg
¼ teaspoon ground cloves

Heat 10g of the 75g coconut oil in a pan, then add the kernels.

Cover the pan immediately with a lid and let the kernels pop, shaking constantly so that they don't burn.

When all the kernels have popped, transfer the popcorn to a bowl.

Pour the remaining coconut oil, coconut palm sugar and spices on top and stir in.

PEANUT BUTTER
MACA FUDGE

Biting into a little square of this gooey fudge is guaranteed to brighten
my day. These are always the treats I offer to one of my closest friends,
Charmaine, if she's a little down. Anything peanut butter puts a smile
on her face, and these have become her best PB snack. With just five
ingredients, they couldn't be more basic, and easy to make.

Makes 16 Fudge Squares

350g peanut butter

65ml date syrup

4–5 tablespoons melted coconut butter or melted raw coconut oil (butter is preferable)

5 tablespoons maca powder

½ teaspoon salt

Mix all the ingredients together in a mixing bowl.

Line a 20cm x 20cm brownie tin with greaseproof paper.

Place the mixture in to the brownie tin, flattening down the
top with your hands or the back of a spoon, and store in the
freezer for an hour.

Remove from the freezer and cut into bite-size pieces.

These are best served straight from the freezer.

RAW CACAO &
PEANUT BUTTER
TRUFFLES

The chocolate and peanut butter combination is always a winner. These truffles are just like a brownie in a ball, and make the perfect afternoon snack.

Makes 16 Truffles

200g peanut butter
100g jumbo oats (interchangeable with millet flakes)
200g soft pitted Medjool dates
4 tablespoons cacao powder, plus extra for rolling
75ml maple syrup
pinch of salt

Place all of the ingredients into a food processor and blend until the mixture comes together.

Roll into balls, roll in the extra cacao powder to coat all over and place in the fridge to firm up.

TAHINI TRUFFLES

If you are a halva fan, then these truffles are for you. The raw honey in this recipe has been chosen because it complements the taste of the sesame so well. One of these balls will be enough to satisfy those sweet cravings, but if you can stop at one, then that is quite some achievement. I certainly can't!

Makes 10–12 Truffles

60g ground almonds
60g tahini
3 tablespoons cacao powder
135g soft pitted Medjool dates
1 tablespoon raw honey
25g white chia seeds

Mix all the ingredients except for the chia seeds together in a food processor until well combined.

Roll the mixture into balls.

Pour the chia seeds into a bowl and then roll the balls in the chia seeds so they are covered.

Place in the fridge to firm up a bit.

These are best when stored in the fridge.

PEAR &
APPLE CRISPS

{ Nut Free }

By thinly slicing across pears and apples and baking them at a low heat, you are able to make the most moreish and naturally sweet snack. I love to make these in large quantities so that they can sit in a large bowl and be picked at by everyone in the house.

Makes a Small Bowl of Crisps

softened coconut oil, for greasing the tray
1 apple (any variety)
1 pear (any variety)

Preheat the oven to 120°C/250°F/Gas mark ½.

Take a paper towel and use it to spread a thin layer of coconut oil on a baking tray.

Very thinly slice the apple and pear, removing any pips as you go. This is easily done using a mandolin or the slicing area on a grater.

Lay the thin slices on the baking tray and bake in the oven for around 40 minutes. The edges will curl slightly and the fruit will become dry. Check after 30 minutes and lift the slices to ensure they don't stick. If you feel they should be a little drier, put them back in the oven until they are cooked. They are ready when they have turned a pale brown.

Cakes

BAKED CARROT CAKE

I absolutely love a moist cake rather than a dry, crumbly one, and carrot cake is one of the gooiest varieties when you get it right. Traditionally, it is the large amounts of butter mixed with the carrot that provides the moisture in a carrot cake, but, since I can't eat dairy, I had to find another way to achieve this. This cake has the ideal level of moisture due to the finely ground almonds and carrot.

Makes an 18cm Double Layer Cake

softened coconut oil, for
   greasing the tins
Cinnamon Cashew Cream
   (page 53)
orange zest, to decorate

CAKE
480g ground almonds
80g buckwheat flour
1 teaspoon ground nutmeg
2 teaspoons ground
   cinnamon
¼ teaspoon salt
240g sultanas
480g carrots, finely grated
zest of 2 oranges
60g melted raw coconut oil
500ml maple syrup

Preheat the oven to 180°C/350°F/Gas mark 4.
Grease two 18cm cake tins.

TO MAKE THE CAKE
Mix the ground almonds, flour, spices, salt and sultanas in a bowl.

Add the grated carrot and orange zest and mix again.

Add the oil and maple syrup and stir to combine.

Spoon the mixture into the two tins, making sure they have equal amounts.

Smooth the top and bake in the oven for 1 hour, checking on them once 45–50 minutes has passed as they may need covering with foil for the remaining time.

Remove from the oven and leave to cool entirely in their tins. When you get them out they will still feel slightly moist in the middle, but they firm up a bit as they cool.

Remove the cake from the tin and ice the top of the first cake with the Cinnamon Cashew Cream, then stack the other cake on top and ice this with more frosting.

Grate the orange zest over the top to decorate and for extra flavour.

LEMON, COURGETTE & POPPY SEED CUPCAKES

The appearance of these cupcakes speaks for itself. Usually a frosted cupcake can be really rich and heavy – these little citrussy beauties, however, are fluffy, light and fresh. I love to serve these for tea.

Makes 12 Cupcakes

softened coconut oil, for greasing
the tins
Lemon Frosting (page 56)

CAKES

3 tablespoons flaxseed
160g coconut flour
40g sprouted buckwheat flour
¼ teaspoon salt
2 tablespoons poppy seeds
40g melted raw coconut oil
100ml maple syrup
juice and zest of 2 lemons
100ml Almond Milk (page 42)
180g courgettes, grated and
strained to remove any
excess liquid

Preheat the oven to 180°C/350°F/Gas mark 4. Grease the muffin tins with the coconut oil or line with muffin cases.

TO MAKE THE CAKES

Mix the flaxseed with 6–9 tablespoons water and leave to set for 10 minutes until a thick, jelly-like consistency is formed. This is known as a flax egg and helps to bind ingredients.

Sift the flours and salt into a bowl.

Add the poppy seeds and then put to one side.

In another bowl, mix together the coconut oil, maple syrup, lemon juice and zest and flax egg.

Pour this wet mixture and the milk into the dry mix and whisk together using a hand whisk.

Add the courgette and stir through.

Spoon the mixture into the greased muffin tins or cases.

Bake for 30 minutes until browning on top.

Once the cupcakes are cool, top with the Lemon Frosting.

BEETROOT & CACAO TORTE

With Beetroot Cream Frosting

Made with red dye and cocoa, red velvet cupcakes have the most beautiful rich red colour and have become one of the world's most popular flavours. Not only did I want to create a recipe that looked as attractive, but I was also really keen to get beetroot (which I adore) into at least one of my recipes. It was important to me, however, that this cake was liked even by those who don't necessarily love beetroot. After my many attempts and sampling sessions, I hope I have managed to come up with a really scrumptious version that everyone will enjoy.

Makes a 20cm Double Layer Cake

softened coconut oil, for greasing
   the tins
2 x Chocolate Avocado Frosting
   recipe (page 57), without the
   cacao and with 1 tablespoon
   beetroot concentrate

CAKE

4 tablespoons flaxseed
330g oat flour
70g coconut flour, sifted
150g melted raw coconut oil
170ml date syrup
150ml maple syrup
3 tablespoons beet concentrate
5 tablespoons cacao powder
80g cooked beetroot, finely grated
2 tablespoons apple cider vinegar
200ml Almond Milk (page 42)
   or Oat Milk (page 44) for a
   nut-free torte
1½ teaspoons vanilla powder

Preheat the oven to 180°C/350°F/Gas mark 4. Grease two 20cm cake tins with coconut oil.

TO MAKE THE CAKE

Mix the flaxseed with 8–12 tablespoons water and leave to set for 10 minutes until a thick, jelly-like consistency is formed. This is known as a flax egg and helps to bind ingredients.

Mix all the cake ingredients in a bowl with a spoon until well mixed and pour into the cake tins.

Bake for 20–25 minutes until firm along the edges and bouncy in the middle.

Leave the cakes to cool completely.

Spread half the frosting on top of the first cake, then place the second cake on top of this. Spread the remaining frosting on top.

HONEY LOAF CAKE
{Nut Free}

Honey cake is a very traditional dessert served during the celebrations of Jewish New Year. The use of honey is significant as it symbolizes a sweet new year. Not only do I love what the honey represents in this instance, but I also absolutely adore the taste. Probably not, however, as much as my eldest sister, Jemma, does. She is obsessed with honey cake, jumping at the opportunity to be the baker of it for each year's Rosh Hashanah dinner. Together, Jemma and I designed this recipe so that there was a honey cake we could all enjoy together for years to come.

Makes 1 Loaf

320g jumbo oats, ground to an oatmeal before using (or 290g ground almonds and 30g buckwheat flour)
250g raw honey
110g coconut palm sugar
75g melted raw coconut oil
juice and zest of 1 big orange
1 tablespoon grated fresh ginger
½ teaspoon ground nutmeg
2 teaspoons ground cinnamon

Preheat the oven to 180°C/350°F/Gas mark 4.

Mix all the ingredients in a mixing bowl with a spoon.

Line a 20cm x 11cm loaf tin with greaseproof paper.

Pour the mixture into the loaf tin.

Bake for 35–40 minutes until the top is golden and slightly cracked.
The cake will cool as it firms, but there should still be a slightly softer, wetter middle.

RAW CARROT CAKE

Carrot is a cake flavour enjoyed across the world. Carrots are naturally sweet and so are an ideal ingredient to use in baking. Although carrot cakes are conventionally baked, raw carrot cakes are equally irresistible, and are not so different from the baked variety. This is moist, dense and packed with flavour.

Makes an 18cm cake

softened coconut oil, for greasing
    the tin
½ Orange Caramel recipe
    (page 61)
10 pecans or walnuts, to
    decorate (optional)
1 teaspoon ground cinnamon, for
    dusting (optional)

CAKE
100g jumbo oats
180g pecans
50g ground almonds
30g ground flaxseed
200g soft pitted Medjool dates
100g dried apricots
200g carrots, roughly grated
juice of 1 orange
1 teaspoon ground cinnamon
½ teaspoon ground ginger
¼ teaspoon ground nutmeg
¼ teaspoon salt
125g raisins

TO MAKE THE CAKE
Blend all the ingredients except the raisins in a food processor until well combined.

Add the raisins and stir in.

Grease an 18cm loose-bottomed cake tin. Pour the batter into the tin.

Cover the cake with the caramel frosting.

Place in the fridge for 1–2 hours to firm.

Decorate with the chopped pecans or walnuts and dust with the ground cinnamon, if using.

RAW LEMON 'CHEESECAKE'

Soaking cashews overnight and blending them with other ingredients creates a mix that can be left to set in the freezer to develop a thick, creamy texture. These raw 'cheesecakes' can be made with so many ingredients, and in my opinion lemons are one of the best to use, giving a refreshing and zesty flavour.

Makes a 24cm Cheesecake

lemon zest, chopped pistachios
   and/or fresh berries
   (optional), to serve

BASE
60g soft pitted Medjool dates
165g unsalted pistachio kernels
90g blanched almonds

LEMON CHEESECAKE LAYER
75g macadamia nuts
85g cashews
75g raw coconut oil
90ml full-fat coconut milk (mix
   the tin well before using)
90ml fresh lemon juice
50ml maple syrup
zest of 1 lemon

Soak the macadamia nuts and cashews overnight or for a minimum of 4–6 hours. Drain and rinse.

TO MAKE THE BASE
Blend all the ingredients in a food processor until they start to come together and then pour into a 24cm pie tin and push down to cover the base.

TO MAKE THE LEMON CHEESECAKE LAYER
Add everything except the lemon zest to the food processor and blend until smooth.

Add the zest and pulse a couple of times.

Pour on top of the base and place in the freezer for a couple of hours to set.

Take out of the freezer at least 2 hours before serving and keep in the fridge.

Serve the cheesecake with a sprinkling of lemon zest, some chopped pistachios and fresh berries, if using.

COFFEE & WALNUT FROSTED CAKE

I don't use walnuts in many of my recipes as they have quite a strong flavour and can be bitter. Coffee and walnut cake is really traditional, so I wanted to play around to see if I could create something yummy... and I did!

Makes a 20cm Double Layer Cake

softened coconut oil, for greasing the tins
Coffee Caramel (page 61)
10–15 walnuts halves, to decorate

CAKE
400g walnut pieces
10g instant coffee, dissolved in 4 tablespooons boiling water
300ml maple syrup
350g oat flour
80ml full-fat coconut milk (the contents of the tin mixed well)
100g melted raw coconut oil, plus extra for greasing
2 tablespoons cacao powder
pinch of salt

Preheat the oven to 180°C/350°F/Gas mark 4. Grease two 20cm cake tins.

TO MAKE THE CAKE
Grind the walnuts in a food processor until a coarse flour is formed.

Combine all the ingredients for the cake in a mixing bowl and stir well.

Divide the mixture evenly between the two cake tins.

Bake for 25–30 minutes, until the top is browned and the cake feels slightly firm to the touch.

Leave the cakes to cool for 5–10 minutes in the tin before moving to a wire rack to let cool completely.

Once cool, use half the Coffee Caramel frosting to cover one cake and place the other cake on top. Ice with the remaining Coffee Caramel. Decorate with the walnuts.

CHRISTMAS COURGETTE CAKE

{ *Nut Free* }

Christmas cakes are enjoyed throughout the world during the festivities. These cakes can vary greatly, so I wasn't scared to experiment with some slightly more obscure ingredients in this one! The mix of courgette, apple purée and spices such as cinnamon, nutmeg and cloves creates a dreamy taste and texture. Although this cake is still quite dense, it is lighter than many of the more conventional Christmas cakes and so there is more likely to be room for this at the end of a big Christmas meal!

Makes an 18cm Cake

softened coconut oil, for greasing the tin

2 tablespoons flaxseed

300g sprouted buckwheat flour

100g coconut palm sugar

100ml maple syrup

100g melted raw coconut oil

340g courgettes, grated with skin on

1 tablespoon ground cinnamon

zest of 2 big oranges

150g sultanas

¼ teaspoon ground cloves

¼ teaspoon ground nutmeg

½ teaspoon salt

1 teaspoon vanilla powder

75g apple purée or unsweetened apple sauce

Preheat the oven to 180°C/350°F/Gas mark 4.

Grease and line a fairly deep 18cm loose-bottomed cake tin with coconut oil.

Mix the flaxseed with 4–6 tablespoons water and leave to set for 10 minutes until a thick, jelly-like consistency is formed. This is known as a flax egg and helps to bind ingredients.

Place all the cake ingredients in a bowl and stir with a spoon until well mixed, then pour into the cake tin.

Bake for 55 minutes, covering with foil for the final 10 minutes.

Remove from the oven, the cake should be firm but still bouncy. Leave to cool in the tin.

RAW LAYERED BERRY 'CHEESECAKE'

My Mum's favourite birthday cake for as long as I can remember was a strawberries and cream layered cake. Each year my Dad would buy her one from their favourite patisserie. My family are all huge supporters of my new lifestyle, often adopting the way I eat, but I was still suprised when my Mum asked me to create a new recipe for her last birthday, replacing her favourite cake. I was excited by this challenge and came up with this raw cashew-layered 'cheesecake'. Seeing how quickly the cake disappeared at her birthday meal filled me with such happiness.

Makes an 18cm Cheesecake

softened coconut oil, for greasing the tin
Sticky Nut Crust (page 49)
fresh berries and coconut flakes (optional), to serve

VANILLA LAYER
500g cashews
125ml maple syrup
2 teaspoons vanilla powder
juice of ½ lemon
120g melted raw coconut oil

STRAWBERRY LAYER
125g frozen strawberries
1 tablespoon melted raw coconut oil
35g strawberries, thinly sliced

BLUEBERRY LAYER
75g frozen blueberries
15g finely desiccated coconut

Continued ››

Grease an 18cm deep cake tin. Press the crust into the bottom of the tin.

TO MAKE THE VANILLA LAYER

Soak the cashews overnight or for a minimum of 4–6 hours. Drain and rinse.

Put all the ingredients for the vanilla layer except the coconut oil in a food processor. Mix well for about 3 minutes until the mixture is really smooth and creamy. Add the coconut oil and mix again.

Separate the mixture into three equal portions.

TO MAKE THE STRAWBERRY LAYER

With a third of the mixture, make the strawberry layer by adding the frozen strawberries and blending again. Add the tablespoon of coconut oil and mix again.

Spoon this mixture on top of the base in the cake tin, and then place the thinly sliced strawberry pieces on top.

Place in the freezer for 30 minutes–1 hour, if you have time, in order to firm it up before adding the second layer.

Once it has firmed up a little, put the second third of the mixture on top of this – the vanilla layer.

Return to the freezer again for 30 minutes to 1 hour.

TO MAKE THE BLUEBERRY LAYER

With the remaining third, return it to the food processor again and add the blueberry layer ingredients, mixing well. Spoon this layer on top of the vanilla layer.

Leave the cheesecake to set in the freezer for 2–3 hours, taking out at least 30 minutes before serving with fresh berries and coconut flakes, if using.

Best stored in the fridge.

CHOCOLATE ALMOND BUTTER CAKE

With Chocolate Frosting

For as long as I can remember, I have always had a traditional chocolate sponge with creamy chocolate icing for my birthday. On the day before my birthday in the year I was diagnosed with all my intolerances, I decided to set myself a challenge and make my own birthday cake for the first time. It did take a few attempts, but I finally got there, and I can safely say that that year I had a better chocolate cake than I had ever eaten before.

Serves 10–12

softened coconut oil, for greasing the tin
2 x Chocolate Avocado Frosting recipe (page 57)
a selection of mixed berries, to decorate

CAKE
500g soft pitted Medjool dates
65g cacao powder
700g almond butter
600ml Oat Milk (page 44)

Preheat the oven to 180°C/350°F/Gas mark 4. Grease two 18cm cake tins.

TO MAKE THE CAKE
Blend all the ingredients in a food processor until well mixed.

Pour the mixture into the cake tins and place in the oven.

Bake for 25–30 minutes until firm along the sides, but still bouncy in the middle. Keep checking as you don't want to over bake.

To assemble the cake, spread half the frosting onto one of the cakes and then place the other cake on top, finishing with the remaining frosting.

Top with your choice of mixed berries. Blueberries, strawberries and raspberries all work well.

Ice Cream

SALTED ORANGE CARAMEL CASHEW ICE CREAM

This recipe uses the Orange Caramel staple recipe, which is swirled through a cashew ice cream. In every spoonful you get an amazingly sticky bit of caramel, which tastes so divine as well as looking beautiful. I love the tanginess of the orange in combination with the sweet cashew cream – it makes it a very refreshing eat.

Serves 8–10

ICE CREAM

400g cashews

400ml tin full-fat coconut milk

3 tablespoons melted raw
    coconut oil

100ml maple syrup

1½ teaspoons vanilla powder

juice of 1 large orange

pinch of sea salt

¾ Orange Caramel recipe (page 61),
    with ½ teaspoon sea salt added
    (or more to taste)

TO MAKE THE ICE CREAM

Soak the cashews overnight or for a minimum of 4–6 hours. Drain and rinse.

Add the soaked, drained cashews, coconut milk, coconut oil, maple syrup, vanilla, orange juice and sea salt to a food processor and blend until creamy and smooth, scraping down the sides as needed. You want it to be completely blended.

Put the ice cream in a freezer-proof container with a lid and place in the freezer for 1–1½ hours.

Take the ice cream out of the freezer and stir it together using a spoon.

Using a spoon or knife, swirl the salted Orange Caramel through the ice cream mixture. Add a pinch of salt for an even more salty-sweet contrast, if desired.

Smooth the top and cover well. Freeze for at least 4–6 hours or until firm.

Take the ice cream out of the freezer 20 minutes before serving to make it easier to scoop.

PISTACHIO ICE CREAM

I was always a lover of pistachio ice cream, and so I was desperate to create my own. This recipe is so thick and creamy and I love the odd crunch of chopped pistachios that you find.

Serves 4

300g cashews
135g coconut palm sugar
165g unsalted pistachio kernels
400ml tin full-fat coconut milk
75g melted raw coconut oil
2 tablespoons Blanched Almond Vanilla Butter (page 46)
½ teaspoon vanilla powder
¼ teaspoon salt

Soak the cashews overnight or for a minimum of 4–6 hours. Drain and rinse.

Grind the coconut palm sugar in a pestle and mortar until you have a powdery consistency.

Grind 115g of the pistachios in a food processor to a fine flour, leaving the remaining 50g whole to stir through at the end.

Blend the soaked cashews in a food processor with the coconut milk, coconut palm sugar, coconut oil, almond butter, vanilla, ground pistachios and salt until totally smooth.

Stir through the whole pistachios. Put the ice cream in a freezer-proof container with a lid and place in the freezer.

After 1–1½ hours, remove from the freezer and mix up with a spoon. Return to the freezer for 4–6 hours.

Take the ice cream out of the freezer 20 minutes before serving.

CHOCOLATE BANANA ICE CREAM

{ *Nut Free* }

By freezing chopped bananas and blending them when frozen, you create a
cold, creamy texture that is amazing to eat then and there and can also be
put back in the freezer to be eaten at a later date. In this recipe, I add cacao
to make a rich chocolate ice cream that still feels surprisingly light. I'd like to
dedicate this to one of my oldest and greatest friends, Rebecca, who has been
dairy intolerant her whole life and has always struggled to find sweet treats.

Serves 4

300g frozen peeled and chopped bananas
3 tablespoons date syrup
5 tablespoons cacao powder

Mix the frozen bananas in a food processer with the other ingredients
and it is ready to serve.

DATE & RAISIN CASHEW ICE CREAM

I took inspiration from the famous Rum & Raisin ice cream, but swapped the rum for date syrup, which gives it a similar colour and an equally rich taste. I can never get enough of this – I could happily get through the whole bowl in one sitting.

Serves 8–10

380g cashews
200ml Almond Milk (page 42)
160ml date syrup
1 teaspoon vanilla powder
2 tablespoons melted raw coconut oil
pinch of salt
60g raisins

Soak the cashews overnight or for a minimum of 4–6 hours. Drain and rinse.

Add everything to the blender except the raisins and blend until smooth.

Fold in the raisins. Put the ice cream in a freezer-proof container with a lid and place in the freezer.

Take out of the freezer after 1–1½ hours and mix up with a spoon. Cover and return to the freezer for 4–6 hours.

Take the ice cream out of the freezer 20 minutes before serving to make it easier to scoop.

Ice Cream Crumble Parfaits

Combining two of my greatest loves, crumble and ice cream, was an absolute must. These parfaits, made with crumble toppings sandwiched between layers of banana ice cream, are little tastes of heaven. I love to serve them in glasses so that the layers can be seen clearly. They are an impressive-looking dessert whilst being incredibly simple to make.

CINNAMON CRUMBLE PARFAIT

If you love cinnamon, this is a recipe you really have to try. The flavours from the banana, cinnamon and crumble topping work so well together.

Serves 4

CRUMBLE LAYERS

145g ground almonds

175g jumbo oats

1 tablespoon ground cinnamon

75ml maple syrup

4 tablespoons melted raw
    coconut oil

BANANA ICE CREAM

6 large frozen, peeled and
    chopped bananas

3 teaspoons ground cinnamon

TO MAKE THE CRUMBLE LAYERS

Preheat the oven to 180°C/350°F/Gas mark 4.

Mix the ingredients for the crumble together and bake on a baking tray in the oven for 8–10 minutes.

TO MAKE THE BANANA ICE CREAM

Blend the frozen bananas and cinnamon in a food processor.

Spoon a little ice cream into each glass first, followed by crumble, and then repeat for four layers.

STRAWBERRY CRUMBLE PARFAIT

This probably wins my vote as my number one summer dessert from the book. It is light, yet perfectly satisfying, and it also looks so beautiful. By mixing berries with the banana ice cream, the banana flavour becomes a little more subtle and a fresher berry flavour is introduced.

Serves 4

CRUMBLE LAYERS

1 tablespoon goji powder

2 teaspoons vanilla powder

155g ground blanched or
   raw almonds

100g buckwheat flakes or
   jumbo oats

3 tablespoons melted raw
   coconut oil

60ml maple syrup

**BANANA AND STRAWBERRY
ICE CREAM**

200g fresh strawberries

470g frozen peeled and chopped
   bananas

1¼ teaspoons vanilla powder

200g fresh raspberries, to layer
   on top

TO MAKE THE CRUMBLE LAYERS

Preheat the oven to 180°C/350°F/Gas mark 4.

Mix all the crumble ingredients in a bowl. Transfer to a baking tray and bake in the oven for 10 minutes.

TO MAKE THE BANANA AND STRAWBERRY ICE CREAM

Add everything to a blender or food processor and blend until you have a soft consistency.

One at a time, spoon the ice cream, raspberries and crumble into a glass or bowl, finishing with some raspberries on top.

Index

A
agave 36
almond butter 27–8
   chocolate almond butter cake 234
almond flour 28
almonds 27
   almond & maca pancakes 77
   almond milk 28, 42
   blanched almond vanilla butter 46
apples
   apple & cinnamon oat balls 78
   apple & gooseberry crumble 161
   apple & raisin sprouted porridge muffins 70
   apple crumble squares 112
   apple mousse 162
   apple pie 141–2
   baked apples with pecans 186
   pear & apple crisps 209
apricot tart 146
avocados
   chocolate avocado frosting 57
   chocolate orange avocado brownies 94

B
bananas 38
   baked cinnamon & banana bars 67
   banana & cacao quinoa bowl 84
   banana & peanut butter crumble squares 113
   banana bread 83
   blueberry & banana oat pancakes 75
   chocolate banana ice cream 241
   raw banoffee pie slab 107
beetroot & cacao torte 218
berries
   berry crumble squares 114
   berry tartlets 152
   raw layered berry 'cheesecake' 231–2
biscuits *see* cookies & biscuits
blueberries
   blueberry & banana oat pancakes 75
   blueberry porridge squares 73
brownies
   chocolate orange avocado brownies 94
   raw frosted chocolate brownies 103
buckwheat flour 25
buckwheat groats 25
butters, nut 46–7

C
cacao powder 25, 27
   banana & cacao quinoa bowl 84
   beetroot & cacao torte 218
   cacao & hazelnut pancakes 74
   cacao & maca popcorn 193
   matcha & cacao truffles 192
   raw cacao & carob sandwich cookies 126
   raw cacao & peanut butter truffles 206
   see also chocolate
cakes
   baked carrot cake 214
   banana bread 83
   beetroot & cacao torte 218
   chocolate almond butter cake 234
   chocolate & orange caramel cake tart 154
   chocolate orange avocado brownies 94
   Christmas courgette cake 230
   coffee & walnut frosted cake 228
   honey loaf cake 221
   lemon, courgette & poppyseed cupcakes 216
   peanut butter & jelly cake squares 88
   raw carrot cake 225
   raw frosted chocolate brownies 103

caramel
  chocolate caramel biscuit fingers 118
  chocolate & orange caramel cake tart 154
  date caramel 61
  oranges in caramel 163
  raw banoffee pie slab 107
  raw chunky peanut butter slab 96
  raw orange caramel slab 95
  salted orange caramel cashew ice cream 238
cardamom, coconut & brown rice pudding 170
carob powder: raw cacao & carob sandwich cookies 126
carrots
  baked carrot cake 214
  carrot oat balls 80
  raw carrot cake 225
cashews 31
  cinnamon cashew cream 53
  date & raisin cashew ice cream 242
  salted orange caramel cashew ice cream 238
  sweet date & cashew butter frosting 51
'cheesecakes'
  raw layered berry 'cheesecake' 231–2
  raw lemon 'cheesecake' 226
chia seeds
  pecan, orange & chia truffles 194
  strawberry jam 58
chocolate
  baked peanut butter chocolate pots 158
chocolate almond butter cake 234
  chocolate & orange caramel cake tart 154
  chocolate avocado frosting 57
  chocolate banana ice cream 241
  chocolate caramel biscuit fingers 118
  chocolate coconut biscuit bars 123
  chocolate malted maca biscuits 120
  chocolate orange avocado brownies 94
  chocolate orange crumble 179
  dark chocolate 54
  mocha mousse tart 150
  peanut butter & chocolate cookies 130
  raw banoffee pie slab 107
  raw chunky peanut butter slab 96
  raw chocolate & maca molten lava cakes 164

  raw frosted chocolate brownies 103
  raw matcha & chocolate slab 91
  raw orange caramel slab 95
  raw tiramisu 167–8
    see also cacao powder
Christmas courgette cake 230
Christmas flapjacks, raw 100
Christmas mince pies 148
Christmas popcorn 202
cinnamon 36
  apple and cinnamon oat balls 78
  baked cinnamon & banana bars 67
  cinnamon cashew cream 53
  cinnamon crumble parfait 245
coconut, desiccated 23
  chocolate coconut biscuit bars 123
  nectarine & coconut crumble squares 111
  salted tahini & coconut fudge 197
coconut butter 22
  all (coconut) butter flapjacks 93
coconut milk 23
  cardamom, coconut & brown rice pudding 170
coconut oil 21–2
coconut palm sugar 34, 36
coffee
  coffee & walnut frosted cake 228
  coffee caramel 61
  coffee shot breakfast balls 79
  raw mocha granola bars 69
  raw tiramisu 167–8
cookies & biscuits
  chocolate caramel biscuit fingers 118
  chocolate coconut biscuit bars 123
  chocolate malted maca biscuits 120
  crunchy ginger cookies 124
  maca & raisin cookies 125
  oat & raisin cookies 128
  peanut butter & chocolate cookies 130
  raw cacao & carob sandwich cookies 126
  raw ginger cookies 135
courgettes
  Christmas courgette cake 230
  lemon, courgette & poppyseed cupcakes 216

cream, cinnamon cashew 53
crispies
    maca quinoa crispies 190
    peanut butter brown rice crispies 200
crisps, pear & apple 209
crumble squares
    apple crumble squares 112
    banana & peanut butter crumble squares 113
    berry crumble squares 114
    nectarine & coconut crumble squares 111
crumbles
    apple & gooseberry crumble 161
    chocolate orange crumble 179
    cinnamon crumble parfait 245
    strawberry crumble parfait 246
    summer peach crumble 172
cupcakes, lemon, courgette & poppyseed 216

D
date syrup 34
dates 34
    date & raisin cashew ice cream 242
    date caramel 61
    quinoa & date crust 50
    sticky nut crust 49
    sweet date & cashew butter frosting 51

E
equipment 38–9

F
fig jam 60
flapjacks
    all (coconut) butter flapjacks 93
    raw Christmas flapjacks 100
flaxseeds 32
frosting
    chocolate avocado frosting 57
    lemon frosting 56
    sweet date & cashew butter frosting 51
fruit 33, 36, 38
    chopped fresh fruit salad 176
    raw fruity granola bars 64

    see also dates; raisins, etc
fudge
    peanut butter maca fudge 204
    salted tahini & coconut fudge 197

G
ginger
    crunchy ginger cookies 124
    raw ginger cookies 135
gooseberries: apple & gooseberry crumble 161
granola bars
    raw fruity granola bars 64
    raw matcha granola bars 68
    raw mocha granola bars 69

H
hazelnuts
    cacao & hazelnut pancakes 74
honey loaf cake 221

I
ice cream
    chocolate banana ice cream 241
    date & raisin cashew ice cream 242
    pistachio ice cream 240
    salted orange caramel cashew ice cream 238

J
jam
    fig jam 60
    strawberry jam 58

L
ladyfingers 167–8
lemons
    lemon, courgette & poppyseed cupcakes 216
    lemon frosting 56
    lemon mousse 182
    raw lemon 'cheesecake' 226

M
maca powder 31
    almond & maca pancakes 77

cacao & maca popcorn 193
chocolate malted maca biscuits 120
maca & raisin cookies 125
maca quinoa crispies 190
peanut butter maca fudge 204
pecan & maca butter 47
raw chocolate & maca molten lava cakes 164
maple syrup 33–4
matcha powder 31–2
matcha & cacao truffles 192
pistachio & matcha balls 198
raw matcha & chocolate slab 91
raw matcha granola bars 68
milks 42–4
almond milk 28, 42
oat milk 44
mince pies, Christmas 148
mocha granola bars, raw 69
mocha mousse tart 150
molten lava cakes, raw chocolate & maca 164
mousse
apple mousse 162
lemon mousse 182
mocha mousse tart 150
raw tiramisu 167–8
muffins, apple & raisin sprouted porridge 70

N

nectarine & coconut crumble squares 111
nougat: raw chunky peanut butter slab 96
nut butters 46–7
blanched almond vanilla butter 46
pecan & maca butter 47
nut & date puddings, sticky 184

O

oat flour 24
the ultimate pastry 48
oat milk 24
oats 24
all (coconut) butter flapjacks 93
apple and cinnamon oat balls 78
apple & raisin sprouted porridge muffins 70

blueberry & banana oat pancakes 75
blueberry porridge squares 73
carrot oat balls 80
oat & raisin cookies 128
oat milk 44
raw Christmas flapjacks 100
oranges
chocolate & orange caramel cake tart 154
chocolate orange avocado brownies 94
chocolate orange crumble 179
orange caramel 61
oranges in caramel 163
pecan, orange & chia truffles 194
raw orange caramel slab 95
salted orange caramel cashew ice cream 238

P

pancakes 74–7
almond & maca pancakes 77
blueberry & banana oat pancakes 75
cacao & hazelnut pancakes 74
parfait
cinnamon crumble parfait 245
strawberry crumble parfait 246
pastry
quinoa & date crust 50
sticky nut crust 49
the ultimate pastry 48
peach crumble, summer 172
peanut butter
baked peanut butter chocolate pots 158
banana & peanut butter crumble squares 113
peanut butter & chocolate cookies 130
peanut butter & jelly cake squares 88
peanut butter brown rice crispies 200
peanut butter caramel 61
peanut butter maca fudge 204
raw cacao & peanut butter truffles 206
raw chunky peanut butter slab 96
pears
pear & apple crisps 209
poached pears 178
pecan butter 31

pecan flour 31
pecans 28
  baked apples with pecans 186
  pecan & maca butter 47
  pecan, orange & chia truffles 194
  pecan pie 139
pies
  apple pie 141–2
  Christmas mince pies 148
pistachios
  pistachio & matcha balls 198
  pistachio ice cream 240
popcorn
  cacao & maca popcorn 193
  Christmas popcorn 202
poppyseeds: lemon, courgette & poppyseed cupcakes 216
porridge muffins & squares
  apple & raisin sprouted porridge muffins 70
  blueberry porridge squares 73
pots, baked peanut butter chocolate 158
pumpkin pie 144

Q
quinoa 32
  banana & cacao quinoa bowl 84
  maca quinoa crispies 190
  quinoa & date crust 50

R
raisins
  apple & raisin sprouted porridge muffins 70
  date & raisin cashew ice cream 242
  maca & raisin cookies 125
  oat & raisin cookies 128
rice
  cardamom, coconut & brown rice pudding 170
  peanut butter brown rice crispies 200

S
salad, chopped fresh fruit 176
salted orange caramel cashew ice cream 238
salted tahini & coconut fudge 197
spices 36

sticky nut & date puddings 184
strawberries
  strawberry crumble parfait 246
  strawberry jam 58, 88
sugar and sweeteners 33
summer peach crumble 172

T
tahini
  salted tahini & coconut fudge 197
  tahini truffles 208
tarts
  apricot tart 146
  berry tartlets 152
  chocolate & orange caramel cake tart 154
  mocha mousse tart 150
  pecan pie 139
  pumpkin pie 144
tiramisu, raw 167–8
torte, beetroot & cacao 218
truffles
  matcha & cacao truffles 192
  pecan, orange & chia truffles 194
  raw cacao & peanut butter truffles 206
  tahini truffles 208

V
vanilla 36
  blanched almond vanilla butter 46

W
walnuts: coffee & walnut frosted cake 228

Thank you

Gosh, it is hard to know where to start here since I attribute so much of my success so far to the people I have been lucky enough to have around me.

Firstly, I would like to thank my family, and foremost, my parents. They allowed me to call and make their kitchen my own. Both of them have helped me in such different ways, but together they provided me with the support and encouragement to start the business and to always keep at it even when it gets tough. Thank you Daddy, for sharing all of your expertise with me, and for your infectious excitement about what the future holds. Your ability to handle and resolve issues when they arise is just one of the many things I hope I have learnt from you. Thank you Mummy, for changing your whole way of life in order for me to be where I am today. For giving up your kitchen for over a year to the kitchen elves, for giving up so much of your time at the beginning to work in hair nets with me chopping fruit, and for always being the most comforting and loyal friend anyone could ever ask for. Thank you Jemma and Hayley, my amazing older sisters who made me who I am today. All the teasing when I was younger just gave me a thicker skin, which is essential when running your own business. Teasing aside (as that is now very much a thing of the past), I also want to thank you for being my best friends and for understanding me when others haven't. You both will always be my favourites.

Thank you Emma and Lydia, my truly special kitchen elves. Livia's Kitchen was able to grow the way it did because of your help, support and reliability and I will always be so grateful to you for that. You and the other lovely elves whom we have met along the way have become such good friends of mine, and working with you and sharing this experience with you has been incredible. Thank you for your true commitment and belief in the company.

Thank you to my wonderful friends, many of whom I have grown up with from a very young age and who have backed every decision I have ever made. Thank you for still being there for me even though this business has meant that I sometimes can't be as social and see you as much as I would like. It is the true friends who you don't have to see or speak to all the time, and I am so lucky to have you all. Thank you also to the friends that I have made on this new and exciting journey. It is so lovely to have made a whole new group of friends from the food world, and I am so happy that we can support and promote each other in the way we do. Ella, a big thank you to you for being so enthusiastic about my business from day one. Some of the introductions you have made have completely changed my life, and I am so grateful to you for that and for many other things.

Thank you Daryl and Alyssia, for being some of the first people to really spur me on to do what I am doing now. Daryl, for your initial interest and the time and advice you have given me throughout my journey. I can only hope to make as much of a success of my company as you did yours, and I am so privileged to have you on board. Thank you Lis, for simply being the most unbelievable friend. Thank you for our Tuesday nights that I couldn't live without, for our early morning spin sessions, and for your unlimited encouragement.

Thank you Jamie, for becoming the rock I needed in the middle of this crazy adventure. Your own passion and drive constantly rubs off on me, which is sometimes just what I need when I am feeling stressed. Thank you for always making me laugh and for all your love.

Thank you to my agent Cathryn, who loved the idea of this book from the first time it was discussed. You have become someone I know I can rely on and trust completely. Thank you also to the team at Ebury, who it has been such a pleasure working with. Lizzy and Louise, thank you for sharing my vision for the book and putting it all together so beautifully. Thank you Tara and Joss, for not only adding to the beauty and the rich feel of the book, but also for the experience and the fun we had together during shooting. I loved those days a lot.

Thank you to Aleksandra, who helped me with writing the sections which required nutritional expertise. You were so generous with your time and taught me so much.

Thank you (and sorry) to my dogs, Cookie and Ruby, who had to move out of home whilst production was carried out. Thank you for loving me just as much when you came home and not holding a grudge.

Lastly, and most importantly, a huge thank you to everyone who has supported me and my company. The amount of encouragement I have received from people I haven't even met never fails to amaze me. I know for certain that I wouldn't be where I am right now without the enthusiasm and backing I have received from you all.

10 9 8 7 6 5 4 3 2 1

Ebury Press, an imprint of Ebury Publishing
20 Vauxhall Bridge Road
London, SW1V 2SA

Ebury Press is part of the Penguin Random House
group of companies whose addresses can be found at
global.penguinrandomhouse.com

Penguin
Random House
UK

First published by Ebury Press in 2016
www.eburypublishing.co.uk

A CIP catalogue record for this book is available
from the British Library

Project editor: Louise McKeever
Design: Miranda Harvey
Photography: Tara Fisher
Food stylist: Joss Herd
Prop stylist: Jo Harris

ISBN: 9781785032271

Colour origination by Rhapsody Ltd London
Printed and bound in China by Toppan Leefung

Penguin Random House is committed to a
sustainable future for our business, our readers
and our planet. This book is made from Forest
Stewardship Council® certified paper.

MIX
Paper from
responsible sources
FSC® C018179